STEP BY STEP WE CLIMB
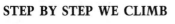
as given by the Ascended Masters

STEP BY STEP WE CLIMB

as given by the Ascended Masters

Volume 1
of the
Step By Step Series

Pearl Publishing
of Mount Shasta

Post Office Box 1290
Mount Shasta, California 96067

Books in this series:

STEP BY STEP WE CLIMB
STEP BY STEP WE CLIMB TO FREEDOM
STEP BY STEP WE CLIMB TO FREEDOM AND VICTORY

These books may be ordered from:

Pearl Publishing
of Mount Shasta
Post Office Box 1290
Mount Shasta, California 96067

See back page for additional information.

Step By Step We Climb (Volume 1)
Text, copyright © 1977 by M.S. Princess.
Cover Art, Pearl Publishing Logo, Step By Step Series Logo,
Introduction, and Subject Index, copyright © 1990 by M.S. Princess.
All Rights Reserved.

Printed in the United States of America.
First printing: 1977   Fourth printing: 1983
Second printing: 1979   Fifth printing: 1985
Third printing: 1982   Sixth printing: 1990

Cover art designed by Cindy and Dewey Reid.

Library of Congress Cataloging in Publication Data

Step by step we climb / as given by the Ascended Masters.
    p.   cm. — (The Step by step series; v. 1)
    A Collection of discourses dictated by the various Ascended
Masters.
    Bibliography: p.
    ISBN 0-9619770-1-9 (pbk.)   ISBN 0-9619770-4-3 (set)

    1. Spirit writings.   I. Series.
BF1290.S72   1990
133.9'3—dc19
                                                              88-18012
                                                                   CIP

A NOTE OF GRATITUDE

I wish to express my deepest gratitude to all the sincere students of the Light whose earnest desire has made the release of this book possible, and to the great Ascended Ones, whose book this is, and whose assistance has been and is unlimited.

—Pearl

DEDICATION

This Book is dedicated in deepest Eternal Love and Gratitude to our Beloved Master Saint Germain, Jesus, the Great Divine Director, the Great White Brotherhood, the Brotherhood of the Royal Teton, the Brotherhood of Mount Shasta, and those other Ascended Masters whose Loving Help and Assistance has been Direct and Without Limit.

The Ascended Master Saint Germain.

INTRODUCTION

"There is only one reality
and that is the living Presence of God within you."

—*Saint Germain*

For centuries in all parts of the world, among all races, in all cultures, there has existed the legend of a mystical brotherhood. The legend describes a secret fellowship, sometimes called the Great White Brotherhood, comprised of individuals who, throughout many lifetimes, have succeeded in mastering all aspects of earthly experience and who have then gone on to serve and assist humanity from a higher dimension, in complete attunement with the One God.

Known for their wise and benevolent use of intelligence, their commitment to serve the good in all men, and the power of their love and compassion, these brothers and sisters have demonstrated the way of perfect development and have ultimately mastered it. Not surprisingly, while in their physical embodiments, these men and women became the beloved Way-showers in their cultures. In the western, Christian world, Jesus and later St. Theresa of Avila were Way-showers. Among eastern traditions, Buddha and Lao Tze were revered as the guardians of the spiritual destiny of the people. In Europe, Saint Germain worked tirelessly to awaken the inner God Presence within the individual.

The written works of these revered saints share a common message: the kingdom of heaven is to be found within the individual. They assert that the experience of the God Presence within is one that can be cultivated, and that it must be cultivated if man hopes to achieve any lasting peace and happiness in this life. When, through meditation, prayer, and other spiritual disciplines, we put our attention on this inner God Presence, we grow into the real purpose of life itself, the joyous experience of unity with God and our fellow men.

You have in your hand a key to the path of development traveled by the saints and the great masters of many traditions. The discourses in this book are given by the Ascended Masters. They are called Ascended Masters because, having mastered human experience, they have ascended this earthly realm and now operate and serve from a higher dimension in God's creation. Unlike those who are called master in various parts of the world, but who function in the physical body, the Ascended Master is no longer physical, but operates in an immortal body made of light. His or Her sole desire and purpose is to serve and assist in illumining and raising the humanity of earth to the level of Mastery.

At appropriate times in every age, the Brotherhood of Ascended Masters delivers some needed instructions to humanity, and one of its own comes forth to perform that service. Some of these events, such as the activity at Lourdes, have been well known and well documented. All have carried a great blessing to the people of Earth, especially to those who have been fortunate enough to experience firsthand the wisdom and love of these emissaries of the Brotherhood.

Another assistance to humanity by the Ascended Masters began in the year 1930. In the late summer of that year, an American named Guy W. Ballard, who later came to be known as Godfre Ray King, decided to spend a few months reviewing and rededicating his life. At this time, Godfre found himself drawn to visit Mount Shasta in northern California, a mountain known for its majestic beauty and for the sanctified atmosphere it radiates. It was his habit to rise early in the morning, and he would then spend the day hiking and exploring. On one of these days, he stopped to take his lunch at a small stream. As he reached his cup into the water, he felt something like an electric current pass through his body, and he suddenly became aware that he was not alone. When he turned around, the Ascended Master Saint Germain stood before him. During the next few months, Godfre was frequently in the blessed presence of the Master. Thus began a course of instruction in which the intimate workings of the great laws of life were revealed to him. This instruction came to be known as the teachings of the Ascended Masters.

The knowledge and practices imparted to Godfre by Saint Germain were a revelation of teachings long held in secret by the Ascended Masters. These were presented in a systematic manner, with each instruction given as a necessary step in the development of the Christ Consciousness and the process of ascension. Saint Germain explained that the student must first accept and then come to experience the God Presence within himself. This inner reality Saint Germain calls the "I AM" Presence. He then gave Godfre instructions how to experience it directly through a technique of meditation, which Godfre describes in his book *Unveiled Mysteries.*

Godfre was then instructed in the unseen laws governing the use of the "I AM" Presence to develop the Christ Consciousness within man. According to Saint Germain, it was by Divine Decree that the men and women of this age should now be shown how to experience the Divine in every phase of human existence and ultimately become free from the wheel of re-embodiment to become Ascended Masters. The time had finally come to remove the shroud of mystery which has always surrounded self-mastery.

Through the application of this knowledge Godfre quickly raised himself to a level of spiritual development seldom seen in the western world. Godfre describes his experience and much of the instruction he was given by Saint Germain in his books *Unveiled Mysteries, The Magic Presence,* and the *I AM Discourses** under his pen name, Godfre Ray King. It was the reading of these experiences, as well as Godfre's humility, love, and divine radiation, that attracted students from all walks of life throughout the world. Of those who were drawn to him, two of his most sincere students were Pearl Diehl (later Pearl Dorris) and Bob LeFevre. Both Pearl and Bob shared a deep desire and a commitment to further the Masters' divine work with humanity. When Godfre's ascension came in 1939, Saint Germain appeared to Bob and Pearl and requested that they render a certain service for him. The depth of their sincerity and dedication over the years had distinguished them to carry on the Master's work. As requested, they assembled a small group of sincere students. It was to this group that Saint Germain and the other Ascended Masters gave the Ascended Master discourses contained in the first two volumes of the *Step by Step Series.*

These are instructions for the attainment of self-mastery. In these discourses the Masters continue to reveal the true under-standing of the spiritual laws of life and how to apply them. They also illumine the most crucial steps we will all take on our path to the Christ Consciousness and our ultimate ascension. In addition, and perhaps most importantly, these teachings are charged with the radiation of these magnificent Beings of Light.

The books in the *Step by Step* series are not the result of "channeling," hypnosis, or any other trance-like procedure. When Saint Germain, or other Ascended Masters would appear, they were visible in their bodies of light to Bob's inner vision. In addition, as the

---

* *Unveiled Mysteries, The Magic Presence,* and the *I AM Discourses* can be ordered from the Saint Germain Press, 1120 Stonehedge Drive, Schaumburg, Illinois 60194.

Masters would speak, letters of light would simultaneously flash before Bob's eyes. This assured tremendous accuracy, not only in recording the information being given, but in capturing the wonderful radiation of love that emanates from these Great Ones.

Volumes I and II contain discourses given by Saint Germain and other Ascended Masters to Bob and Pearl during their years of collaborative service from 1940 to 1949. Volume III is a collection of inspired talks given by Pearl in the 1970's and early 1980's in the living room of her home in Mt. Shasta. These have been transcribed from taped recordings and offer a keen insight into the practical application of the Ascended Master teachings from one who has been practicing them for over fifty years. When once asked to describe the source of the wisdom and insight that poured forth from her during these talks, Pearl answered that it was the result of deep attunement to the "raised consciousness of the Christ Principle."

Under the Masters' guidance, people from all parts of the world have found their way to Pearl's door. Literally thousands have come to listen and ask questions. In Pearl's presence one feels the love and humility of the Christ Consciousness radiating from her being. Her life has been one of dedicated service, and her time and effort has always been given freely and as a gift of love. Such service to mankind, based upon individual effort, is the cornerstone of the Ascended Master teachings and has been the focus of Pearl's life.

It is now possible for all of us to become the example of transcendent love and compassionate service that is our true destiny and the destiny of all those who would walk in the footsteps of the Masters. In the words of Saint Germain:

Yours is the responsibility of your world—yours alone.
Accept the responsibility in joy and happiness, with your
feelings calm and determined, going forward. And I assure
you, never will you lack for any good thing, and you will find
the way opening before you and Ascended Master Friends
springing up to stand by your side."

It is our deepest hope that the teachings and Divine radiation of this book will help all those who have been guided to its message to fully realize this blessed invitation.

CONTENTS

Editorial Note

These discourses were received by Bob LeFevre as a steady stream of Letters of Light flashed before his inner vision by the Masters. As Bob received each discourse, he would read the words aloud. Sunny Widell, the editor of this volume, listened carefully and recorded each discourse verbatim in shorthand as Bob spoke the words. The only indications Sunny received of proper punctuation were the natural pauses in Bob's speech. Punctuation was reconstructed and revised as necessary, hours or days later when Sunny transcribed her shorthand notes.

The transcribed discourses were held by Pearl and Sunny as a sacred trust in their original form for many years until the prompting was received to publish them in a form suitable for the inspiration and guidance of new and developing students. Each discourse was reviewed and all passages of a private, personal, or historical nature were deleted, leaving only the Master's instructions on Divine Law and its application. Occasionally a chapter on a particular subject or point of law was created by compiling relevant paragraphs and passages from different discourses. This editorial process naturally resulted in some compromise to the smooth flow of the original discourses.

Dear reader, if you encounter an occasional error in grammar or punctuation, or if you find a paragraph that does not appear to flow as smoothly as the preceeding material, the editor asks for your patience and understanding. She has done her very best to preserve for you this priceless instruction free from human interference.

I

MAN–A RAY OF LIGHT
by Kuthumi.

From the very Heart of Creation, the Great Central Source, comes forth a Ray of Light. This Ray of Light manifests itself in space as a Flaming Heart of Love and from it in two directions come forth the outpicturing and the outer action of love. Divided in space, the one ray becomes two, and blazing ever onward and outward, eventually forms into the physical bodies of man and woman. Brought forth in Love, living in Love and returning again in time, having expressed all Love, into the fullness of the Love from whence it came. And thus is every individual upon this planet a child of the One God, a being born of a Ray. The ray itself is Love in Action, and upon that ray he is guided through all outer world experience. Thus the individual moves, never even for a moment apart from his Source, for he cannot part from his source inasmuch as he is a part of that Flaming Central Sun from whence he came.

Thus, as one enters the consciousness that "I AM All Things," he will come more clearly to observe that I AM not only all things manifested, but all things unmanifested. I AM all things which I wish to be. I AM all things which I AM. I AM one with the Great Central Sun. I AM the Ray of Light that comes forth from the Heart of God. I AM my body, my mind, my feelings, my entire world in Perfect Harmony, in perfect action together.

There is but one Source of Light, one source of Power, one source of Wisdom, and that One Source is I AM, or Love in Action. Force everywhere acting, whether the force be qualified constructively or destructively, is Love, for all force comes about as a result of attraction or repellence. And either attraction or repellence is the activity of Love, for Love is Light and God, and the same power which brings individuals together or egos together to create a form, or forms together to create a thing, that same force in reverse action will put individuals apart; will separate the atoms; will separate the things; yet both in the action of drawing together and the action of drawing apart is the full expression of Life or Love.

Love expresses itself constantly throughout the universe. It is the power that builds all things, and it is the power that maintains those things operating at any given speed of vibratory action. It is the vibratory action itself, and it is the very substance of which all things are composed. In a complete understanding of love you will readily see that I AM All Love, and therefore, I AM All Things. Again, Love being all things, I AM that I AM. To live with that unlimited consciousness is to raise yourself quickly into the Arisen state.

I wish you to understand very clearly at this point that while there are many Arisen Beings who are above all human consciousness, or lack of love consciousness, there are no Perfected Beings who are above the obedience to the Law of Love.

The impression has been given many times by various ones in various schools of thought that the Arisen Masters are not only quite powerless, but many times actually detrimental to the progress of the human race. To us that seems to be one of the most grievous errors which man can make, for to be taught in any way that there is a great chasm, a great separation between your humanity of this Earth and Ourselves, who are the natural product of perfection released here upon this Earth, is to divide the activity of God, one part against another, and while that may come forth as a temporary expression of love, still indeed it is by the drawing power of Light that each accomplishment is gained. Thus, if one maintains a limited consciousness one will see about him only those things of the appearance world and will be able to see only good and evil. If one will maintain the Limitless Consciousness, he will have entered into the heart of himself, the I AM of each one. From that point he will quickly see that only Divine Order and Divine Love can manifest.

To accept that there is a power other than God, Good, is to give power to the appearance world. Should you observe any individual anywhere performing some act or saying some word that does not appear to be perfection, then it is your obligation, as a student of Life, to refuse acceptance of that inharmonious or negative appearance and know with all the power of your being that there is only God, I AM, Good, acting in that individual. That is law. That is *the* Law. That law has not changed. It can never change. It is the exact law that has built this universe and that shall continue to build it and expand it as long as the human forms that now exist have either disappeared or been raised into the fullness of life, for the Law is: there is only One Thing, only One Power, only One Action, and that is Love.

To set Love into action consciously is to agree with the creative principle of all life. To send forth a feeling or a ray of Divine Love before you always is to move freely through a world of many appearances untouched by any of them. All things for good can be accomplished when the individual will love enough. The beloved children of Earth need the release of Divine Love more at this hour than ever before in the history of man upon this planet. It is not so much the understanding that is needed; it is not so much the power to discriminate, but more than any one thing it is the release of Love in Action to flow forth without judgment, without discrimination, but just to flow forth. It is the only power that can raise mankind out of its present appearance of limitation, out of its appearance of destruction and chaos which it has created for itself.

These words which I speak are not new. Humanity has had this Truth given to them many times, particularly in the last few years. The attention of the individual has been brought to this Great Law, but because individuals will not turn and follow that Law, little permanent progress is made. Permanent progress can only come when love is poured forth to the Source of Love, for then the anchoring takes place and that which is in the physical world is permanently decreed or willed into manifested form.

All things that exist are consciousness. All things that have now definite form are the result of I AM Consciousness.

Another attempt is being made to turn mankind's attention to the Law and not to individuals. The teaching that only through certain channels can the Truth be given is not true, for the Truth is universal in scope and may come forth from the mouth of a child or from the lips of one who appears to be very aged. The Truth, which is the real Light for all the ages that have been and all the ages which are to come, exists correspondent with those ages, and is the Light and the Truth that guides man constantly through the miasma of time and space. I AM *is* the Truth. That Truth does not belong to one group of people, to one sect, to one nation. That Truth belongs to each one, and that Truth must be expressed by each one according to the Light within him.

Tremendous service has been rendered by those who understand the Law of One, which is the Law of Love; but when, through intellectual reasoning that law is forgotten and the attention is constantly turned to the appearance world or the unstable shifting sands of physical things, regardless of what excuse is given, the individual is not following the Law of One, but rather is giving power to the appearance world and thus permitting the law of reaction to take place. Though this law also is the activity of love, still, it is the tearing apart that something new may be built. Only by entering into and being the fullness of the One Law, the One God, I AM, can the individual or the nation escape from the destruction that always precedes a new birth. The new birth is coming and if sufficient of mankind will cease to look to the outer but will indeed enter into the stillness, the Great Silence within, and there become one with the One Law—Love—then this transitory period from the darkness into Light will take place with the quiet beauty of the unfolding petals of a rose.

Everywhere about you, you will observe individuals being stirred up to resent this, to resent that, to fight for this, to battle against that, but that is not the Law of Life, for the Law of Life is Love, and since all things that are contain love, then it is not a part of love to set one portion of love against another. No individual has a right to command what another individual shall do. In the establishing of the new order of things, only by the power of love shall you be governed, and that power of love, if correctly expressed, will turn the individual back constantly to his Source.

The I AM instruction which Saint Germain has brought forth and which We have all assisted in releasing to the children of Earth, must be established and maintained as the highest pinnacle of illumination and love upon this planet. This cannot be done by intolerant outbursts of misqualified energy. It can only be done by entering into the Oneness, the fullness of Divine Love in Action, which is the first Ray coming forth from the Great Central Sun. Although that ray has been divided, still must it come together again, and actually there is no division, but the appearance of division exists that greater love may be expressed.

Love is growth, or, as We prefer to call it, expansion.
It is the constant releasing of Light within the individual
to break from the old and enter ever into the new. There
is one thing that is definitely against the law of expansion
and that one thing is the deplorable conception which
permits individuals or groups of individuals to feel that
that which they have is the only or the total knowledge
which is necessary to the progress of humanity. In My
position I have beheld the activity of religions and
philosophies in every nation and I have observed how re-
lucant is the individual everywhere to accept his Divine
Authority, his Divine Responsibility, and make his
own call to his own I AM Presence that he may find his
own place in the cosmic order of all things. Individuals do
not like to pry themselves loose from the old, and yet
that Light within them is a compelling force which
compels and commands that their expansion does not
stop, that they go forward into the greater and ever
greater, bringing forth newer things, more glorious things,
more illumined things, to be a blessing to themselves and
others.

It is not possible for anyone to put a fence around
the I AM. To build a fence is clearly to indicate that two
forces are acting. There is in reality but One Force; how
then can two forces act? That One Force is Love, Light,
God. From that oneness all things come forth and into
that oneness all things return. Since all things are
consciousness, to maintain the "I AM All Things"
consciousness is to have entered through the Open Door
which no human opinion, no human condition, no
human organization can shut.

Churches, schools, lodges, teachings of one sort or
another must bow before the expansion of the greater
Light within the individual of the New Golden Age, for
that Light is mighty, it knows no opposite, it
acknowledges nothing but itself, for it is One with Itself,
and the individual who carries that Light in this New
Golden Age moves a Great Blazing Beacon of Love and

Blessings always. Regardless of what is said of such a one, that one always moves forward, never taking issue, never choosing sides, for the Master Christ of each one does not recognize issues or sides but always sees clearly through recognizing each problem as an opportunity to expand more of itself, more of its Light.

The Master Mind within each one does not say: "this individual has thwarted me," or "that situation is one which must be removed," but rather does that Master Mind, the Higher Consciousness, observe clearly through all things, seeing only the One and True Principle of Life which I AM. Seeing only that One, every situation, every individual is but the open doorway to greater expansion and to a greater outpouring of Divine Love.

Many do not know how to release Divine Love, for to many the consciousness has been given that Divine Love is an attribute of the physical senses, and I assure you that is not so.

Divine Love is the All-enfolding Flame of Creation, it is the Spark of Life, the Unfed Fire within each one which can be kindled into a roaring conflagration when the attention is turned within and above to the Blazing God Presence, I AM, for that Blazing Presence *is* Love, and only from the Heart of All Love can more love come forth.

Thus, to bring any given thing into manifestation, the individual who will stop, turn, and recognize the I AM within him, will cause a ray of Light to proceed from his mind, which will form the mental picture of that which he desires. And holding that picture consciously in his mind, still within the I AM Consciousness, he will call forth another ray of Light from his feeling world, pouring it into that mental picture which he has held, so that he directs the electronic stream from his Godself to bring about the creation of anything he desires.

To desire is to accept that there is only the One, for desire is the activity by which the One expands into greater and greater Oneness. Without desire, there is only death. The individual who claims to have lost desire is building destruction for himself; however, the individual who refuses to govern his desire has released destruction upon himself. Desire is the action of the mental and feeling worlds combined, which will invariably produce definite, accurate results. To raise desire into the Oneness of Divine Love is to live for one purpose only and that is to be of service, to thy God-self first, and then to all other portions of thy God-self, regardless of the appearance or the temporary form in which that God-self, I AM, may be manifesting at the moment.

To desire things for oneself is to accept that there are two forces acting. In the desire to give service one should lose himself so completely that he becomes selfless. If there be any trace of desire to benefit oneself in service, then that service to that degree will not succeed. The individual must be willing to pluck out of his desire world all things that deal with himself as an individual. He must become Cosmic in his comprehension, and entering into the Oneness, which is the I AM Presence, he will become completely One with all things, and thus be able to serve without desire for self. To be unselfish is really only one action of being totally selfless, for only in the selfless state does one become the I AM principle enfolding all.

Say many times: I AM Light! Light! Light! I AM Love! Love! Love! I AM God! God! God! I AM that I AM that I AM. Thus is the three times three expressed.

To live is to give. To give worthily is to have disciplined yourself so that there is no self but only the great principle "I AM" within each gift. Then to give is to Live Eternally.

Go forward! Sing the Anthem of all Creation. Be the I AM in I AM always. Seek not to establish an outer world authority, but turn each one within himself, that the New Race of God Beings may be quickly established. Seek not for power nor for authority, but seek within that you may put aside all human things and thus know thyself that the Truth will set you free. Be harmonious and happy in all that you do, and never fail to pour forth Divine Love. It will clear the way before you, for it is the One Power that *Is*.

*   *   *

O Thou Ever Present Living Substance of Life, Thou Divine Christ, the I AM Principle of every individualized Flame of God, humbly do we acknowledge Thy Oneness, Thy Mighty Power of Light in Action. Obediently do we accept only Thee, for Thou art All in All. Let Thy Mighty Myriad Rays of Love encircle mankind and raise each one into Thy Oneness.

II

ORDER—THE FIRST LAW
by El Morya

One of the first and most important steps which the seeker upon the pathway of Light must take is that step which leads him to the understanding of the Oneness of all things. Everything in the manifested state or in the unmanifested state is actually consciousness. By manifestation here I mean simply manifestation as a physical thing or substance in the physical world. Knowing, therefore, that all things are consciousness and all things are one, each student must quickly realize that the acknowledgment of the Inner Flame of Life within himself, I AM, God in Action, will automatically have a powerful effect on all of God's creation everywhere; for it is impossible for immediate action to take place anywhere in the universe without an equal reaction somewhere sometime. This is as true in the outer physical realm as it is from the inner, and thus mankind finds himself ruled by an Absolute Law of Cause and Effect, action and reaction.

If the sincere student will think well upon this and accept the responsibility which is his, governing his every thought and feeling, his every spoken word, his every action, he will become a Radiating Sun of Kindness, a

20

Radiant Heart Center of Love, and thus, that which he pours forth as action gathers more of itself and returns as a great reaction of blessing to him always. If he will be so foolish as to send forth in his radiation that which is unkind, critical or condemnatory, or any of the other lower rates of vibratory action in thought or feeling, that one will reap the results just as surely as he sends forth those things. Understanding Love, Light, God, I AM, as being one and the same, makes it possible for the individual to enter sufficiently into the fullness of Light from his Presence.

Once the student learns to turn within himself and then, as his inner consciousness unfolds, look about him, he will have entered the realm of precipitation, the realm of actuality, for he will have left the false world of appearances.

The first rule has always been to be silent and know that I AM is God. This silence will permit the individual to turn within himself, and the knowledge, the vision, the contact with his Presence will quickly follow.

I say to the student always: There is nothing so important as your own harmony and peace of mind. You cannot acquire that from others; that comes only as a result of your own earnest desire and longing for the glories of life, for the outpouring of Light from your own Great God-self, which is within and above you.

I assure you that it is possible for every sincere student who will meditate sufficiently upon that statement to quickly see his own Glorious God Presence, the Great I AM, and also become increasingly aware of the assistance the Arisen Masters are able to give.

To dwell within oneself in perfect calm, in perfect serenity, in perfect majesty, yet with the full power of Divine Love in action flowing forth, is mastery, and that consciousness, that activity sustained, will surely take each one into the victory of Life which each one so longs for. The Arisen state, which all must reach, must be reached consciously; it is a matter of energy released. It

might seem that an individual could become an Arisen
Master without much previous preparation, but I wish to
inform those who hear My voice, or those who will read
these words, that although a student may become arisen,
he is not Master until he earns that right, and the earning
of that right he must accomplish himself.

The only reason for life expressing in the physical
world is to expand more Light. That expansion we have
called service, and that service begins with the love of the
God Flame within, first, and then a love of the God
Flame within all manifested things, second. Yet, even
though we say that one is first and one is second, still,
really they are both first, for when the individual turns
within himself sufficiently and gives the gratitude, the
love, and the adoration to his I AM Presence, he is in
reality loving the Presence of Life within all things, for
all is One.

All substance throughout the universe is
consciousness, or Light, and this Light consciousness
moves in great streams of force at the direction of any
and every individual who can and will say "I AM." To say
"I" is to acknowledge your own individuality, to
acknowledge that you have existence, to acknowledge the
place of your existence, and to say "I AM" is to release
the Full Power of Light, of Light Consciousness
throughout the universe, which may be used according to
the direction given it by the inner understanding of the
one making the call.

No permanent achievement can ever be made in the
physical octave without balance. Balance is the law of the
universe. Order is the first law. Thus, the sincere student
of life will learn to fit all parts of his life into a perfect
pattern so that it expresses order at all times. The
individual who seems to have difficulty in maintaining
order in his personal experiences, his personal daily
habits, is not one through whom the Arisen Masters can
work to good advantage. Even though he may have
remarkable talents in a certain direction, still, unless

balance is maintained, unless Order is his Law of Life, the perfect balance of the Arisen Master may not be released through him in its fullness.

To be trivial is to be extremely human. When there are many vast and serious things confronting you, it does not pay to be trivial. The individual must always have a clear sense of values, putting first, of course, his own Infinite God-self, then the God-self of each one, not according to his personal likes and dislikes, but all as one. "Love thy neighbor as thyself," is this portion of the Law applied.

To observe imperfection in another is a certain indication that you yourself have not reached your goal. Each one's duty is to see most of all the perfection which everyone should have. Even though your outer sight may deny that that perfection is there, still, since only the Inner is real, you will quickly see that the perfection which should be there is there. It is your duty, your obligation as a part of life, to expand that perfection. As that perfection expands there is less room for imperfection. To call the I AM Presence into action to release perfection into any person, place, condition or thing is the greatest possible blessing that can be given. As the pressure of perfection increases, all things unlike that perfection cease to exist. You do not have to destroy darkness. When there is enough light the darkness just ceases to exist. Thus, you never have to observe the imperfection in another. See only the Light, and expand that, for when there is enough Light there the imperfection will cease. To discuss the seeming inabilities, shortcomings, and failures of your acquaintances is to draw those qualities into yourself, and also it intensifies them in the worlds of the others.

Criticism and gossip are the two most active and powerful forces at work for the destruction of mankind at the present time. There is only one way to stop gossip and criticism and that is to stop it! Many times those who sincerely wish to do the right thing feel that under certain conditions on certain occasions conversation concerning another is quite all right. This is not the case. Conversation concerning another, unless it be a blessing to the other, is never a constructive activity. Obedience to that law will quickly bring your world into order.

To know, to feel, to live in, to be the I AM Consciousness all the time is to open the door to your Eternal Freedom. Not only that, but that consciousness maintained will keep that doorway open for yourself, and your progress gained at the expenditure of your own energy may never be taken from you. Even though the radiation of the directing Master may be withdrawn for a time, should the turmoil of an individual in an emotional upheaval bring it about, still that radiation may come forth again and yet again, for We who serve as Elder Brothers of mankind never weary in our service to the children of Earth. Always are We patient, always are We kind, always forgiving. The teaching that one can fail permanently is not true. There is no permanent failure anywhere. The only thing that approaches that is the willful refusal on the part of any individual to release energy or to make his own application.

The greater the power an individual has in his use, the greater humility there should be moving hand in hand with that power, for power without the balancing humbleness required is but a force which will always destroy, even though it may in time bring about much good.

Since it is our province to bring Perfect Balance, Perfect Light, Perfect Understanding and Activity to the weary and bewildered children of this planet, I wish them to have these words of Mine. I AM is the Life within every form. To be able to say a thing, or feel I AM is to accept the responsibility you have to life. Accepting that responsibility in joy, in happiness, without concern or worry, will enable you quickly to expand that life and you will begin to live what has been called "more abundantly."

To determine for himself whether or not the I AM is for any individual, let the one in search of Truth become very still, turn his attention within himself, become conscious of the Light that fills his being and world, and then turning his attention upward, let him recognize and give unending adoration and praise to the source of that Light, the infinite Presence, I AM. This exercise, maintained over a period of time, will release the individual permanently from consideration of the outer human activity and he will find himself moving in a world apart, giving of his great love to all with whom he comes in contact. This is your obligation.

*   *   *

O Thou Glorious, Mighty, Everlasting, Eternal One, Thou Quenchless Flame, Thou Brilliant Sun, beat forth on Thy slender piercing Rays of Power the Understanding of Life that it may penetrate the minds, the feelings, the worlds of individuals everywhere. Mankind, if they are to survive, must know and claim I AM.

III

GUIDE POSTS

by various Masters.

Man in his activity on this planet is a spiritual being first, and a physical being second. The spiritual quality of man has never been fully defined, for the majority of mankind, through long centuries has forgotten his connection with his Source of Life and has come to think of himself as something quite apart, each individual being separate from the other. This is not the case, for man individually and en masse is but One, and only in the heart can the individual accept the oneness, for it is in truth "the Oneness of all things."

Do not let your attention be held by some imperfection that is either in your world or another's, whether it be a physical thing, a mental thing, or an emotional thing. Remove your attention from imperfection! Remember, the law always has been that what your attention is upon you draw into your own world, and the manifestation of the imperfection will be there unless you learn to remove it and see only the perfect thing you would have, and have your world become. This is so easy when you once understand your Source, that your connection with God is within; when

26

you understand that you are first, a spiritual being, a manipulator of Light, of Love, of Power, rather than a physical form conscious only of lack. Know always:

I AM that which I wish to become.
· I AM the fulfillment of my destiny here on earth.
I AM the Victory of Light itself.
I AM the Commanding Presence moving in and
    Conquering everywhere I move.
I AM the Victory of Life over death.
I AM that I AM.

This consciousness, this at-one-ment with your Source, is simply attaining the desire for one-pointedness. It is more difficult to attain when individuals are permitting their attention to stray from one type of imperfection to another. See the perfection you wish to become. Hold your attention upon this, and let the energy of life which flows through you make it a reality!

Forces

In dealing with individuals, remember always that never do you actually have to deal with the individual but always with the force acting through him. And remember too, that when you confront anyone, you are confronting one who will one day become a Master, who is even now upon the pathway. Therefore, if there is anything within that individual which does not please you, then there must also be something in your own world which is not as it should be, and it is your great pleasure, through the power of your love and radiation, to assist in raising him from the force that is operating through him.

But this above everything else: regardless of what force you may see acting in another, make yourself so masterful that you raise that individual out of any force or any activity that may be less than perfection. If you have no personal desires of your own you will find it very easy to do that. When your desire is sincere in helping another, the way is open.

There is only one possible solution to all these adverse forces which man has generated, and that is absolute determination on the part of each and every one to turn his attention to the God within and to remain harmonious; to keep his attention upon things that are constructive, and to be silent. That, of course, is the imperative thing—*to be silent.* O, My precious ones, the amount of energy that is wasted in a single day by almost any one of you through just plain, ordinary not being silent. Could you see from the inner standpoint you would be quite amazed. Learn to be silent!

Use your Wall of Light, your Wall of Protection dynamically, earnestly, and when you find a force beginning to act, instantly call on the Fire of Forgiveness and rebuild your Wall of Light. Call your Presence to make that Wall of Light absolutely invincible, and then you will positively free yourself from inharmonious, doubtful, negative conditions. You must make your application more powerful than the force directed at you; and I am suggesting that you make the call that all interference with yourself be stopped irrespective of where that force comes from.

Do not seek to discriminate against one another, and do not try to find out where projections come from, or if there is some channel who has unknowingly opened himself so that a force is acting in your midst. That is no concern of yours. Call to your Presence not to reveal where the force comes from but to take your attention off it. Too much attention has been given in that direction. You need more of God and less of the human. You are never dealing with human beings; you are dealing with forces, and if a force is about to strike at you through an individual, do not blame the individual. It could not act in your world unless you gave it power, because it has no power of its own. You are master of your world in a few minutes if you will practice this seriously. Take your attention off human beings and become one with your Presence, and thus an Arisen Master. There is no other way. Either follow these rules and become master of your Inner world that you can have greater perfection in the outer world, or go on in the line of least resistance to catastrophe.

When you in your consciousness, through the activity of your feeling world—which is, of course, a part of your consciousness—become aware of a force acting, be certain that you qualify it with perfection, that you accept it as perfection, and should your attention remain upon it more than a few seconds, be consciously aware of an expansion of Light, for I tell you truly when I say that if you will do this you will set up an automatic protection that acts in your feeling world and your consciousness to guard you against the destructive force released by other individuals. Whenever you observe something taking place, qualify it with perfection; that way you send forth only perfection, and as a result that which you send forth will in time manifest in your world.

Always remember in your calls to the I AM Presence that you never have to deal with human beings; always you are dealing with forces, and when you have the prompting, or what seems to be a prompting to step in and, as you sometimes say, give somebody a piece of your mind, instead get by yourself and call the Presence into action to sweep Its Power in and through your world and that of any individual or disturbing condition.

Self-Justification

One of the great enemies to the progress of the individual is self-justification. It is one activity of being dishonest with life. O how many there are, precious students too, as well as those ignorant of the Law, who, when they find there has been some mistake acting in their world or when they find they have committed an error they did not intend to commit, the reaction is instantly to begin to justify what they have done. Is it not amazing that man has not learned that the only reason for life is to learn more about life, so that you can call it forth into perfection? When you discover that you as an individual have made a slight error or done something which you know to be against the Law, rejoice and do not try to find excuses for yourself. Rejoice that you know the Law, that you can give obedience to the Law, call on the Fire of Forgiveness, rejoice, and go on. Never try to say, "if such and such had not been the case this mistake would never have occurred." Of course it wouldn't, but that has nothing to do with you.

Your obligation is to perfect your own world, and you can never perfect your own world so long as you attempt to justify mistakes which seem to creep into the activities of your everyday life. This constant desire on the part of human beings to refuse to admit that they could ever make a mistake is one of the things that keep them making mistakes.

You must recognize from the human standpoint that as long as you operate in the physical octave error is bound to creep in. Perfection only exists in the Arisen state, in the octave of Light. That is why it doesn't make any difference how enlightened a human being may be, so long as the individualized consciousness remains focused in the outer world in any way it is possible for error to creep in. Knowing that and understanding the law in connection therewith, it is so easy to see how ridiculous it would be for any human being anywhere to delude himself into feeling that he could not make a mistake, yet that is just exactly what happens time after time after time. As you value your progress be honest with life!

All things are possible to the one who stands with the Light. Can you not see that the only thing that stands in your way is your human self? There is no obstacle other than that. You, as the I AM Presence, have complete authority. Then why not take that authority, grasp the reins, the Scepter of Dominion, firmly in your hand and command the human to give obedience. Say: "Be still and know that I AM is the Master here." Is it not a magnificent thing to realize that all things can be accomplished when you love enough, and when that Love and Adoration is poured forth, first to the Presence in acknowledgment of the Great Source of Life, and then poured forth indiscriminately to all Life, the doors of the universe stand wide and you may travel where you will, fully protected.

The Law of The One

The Law of the One is the Law of Love. As you go forward do you not see that there is no time or space? We are this moment here actually experiencing the same thing that we will be experiencing in what you choose to call the future, and just as surely as we are gathered here together, the day will come when humanity will be gathered together likewise. Since there is no time, actually there is only *now*—that day is this day, and this day can be expanded into that day. When you comprehend the full meaning of this you will understand the Oneness of all things; you will see there is not growth, but progress; Life is expanding, it is a Flame that goes out in all directions. Thus, the Spark is perfect, and the Fullness of the Flame is perfect, and the expansion between the Spark and the Flame is in reality the Life expanding itself in Perfection. And as you recognize that the Spark and the Flame are One, and the Flame and the Spark are One, you will see your relationship to the Mighty Presence, your relationship to each other, and the inevitability of your own ultimate Victory.

Service

Please remember, in order to learn to discuss an activity for action you must learn to put the human completely out of the picture and stand by, calling the Presence into action to see where you may be of service. Let that service be the watchword, then the way will be open and a magnificent thing will come forth. You cannot afford to let anything, no matter how important it may seem to you personally, even for a moment to stand between you and the service you might render another. Always remember, however, in service you do not help another unless you teach him to help himself.

Man must determine individually and collectively to refuse acceptance to those things which are less than the Perfect Plan of the Great Presence of Life. The Perfection of Life is self-apparent. The imperfection of human understanding is also self-apparent. The only way to raise the human understanding to a point where the Perfection of Life fills it is for the human understanding to increase in vibratory action to the point where the understanding ceases to be human and becomes Divine. This is a very simple matter for the trained student of Light. It is also very simple for anyone who is sincere and wishes to move forward constructively for the balance of his human experience.

Remember, you are in the service of the Great Ones, you are in the service of Life Itself. Never once is there the slightest temptation to turn aside from service to others. True service to Life, your I AM Presence, is true service to Life no matter how it manifests; therefore, your service to others is true service to God, for as you give to the God Presence of each other you fulfill the Great Law. Pour forth your Love to the I AM Presence first, then to the Presence of all life no matter where you find it. When you obey one of those laws you obey the other. Service, dear ones, is Love, for Love is the Essence of all Life, and it is Life. Take time to Love.

Every time you reach out your hand to assist another brother in the Light you are rendering service, and as you render service your consciousness expands. Did you know that? Think about that for a moment. As you release your energy in service to others, particularly to others who serve the Light, your consciousness expands, you acquire greater understanding, greater peace, greater poise, greater skill, and you are applying the Law of Love, and an expansion of your consciousness must take place.

He who sincerely in his heart serves Life, the Great I AM Presence and the Great Host of Arisen Masters, is repaying his debt to Life and assisting all mankind according to the power of the Light which is drawn forth. Yet is it not ridiculous that man feels he must lean upon others, when the very Light that beats his heart, the very power by which he turns to lean upon someone is the Limitless Power of God, I AM, which fills him and should make him a Radiant Being of God's Power.

If your desire is to serve many, to serve the Light, to serve humanity, to raise them into a place where they may also assist others in being finer, cleaner, better individuals—if that alone be your motive—then you are indeed fortunate, for nothing can harm you. But if there is even one unknown thing, perhaps a lurking desire to profit at the expense of another, a desire to take credit, a desire for gain, for power and authority or any such thing, I tell you plainly that your desire will turn to gall within you and the very thing that you desire most will be taken from you. If there is even unknown to you jealousy at the progress of another, watch, for you will have difficulty in maintaining your progress. If you have desire to command with authority, even though that desire may be partially unknown to you, watch, for you will never command with authority as long as that desire remains. If you have desire to profit at the expense of another, watch, and see others profit at your expense.

Guide Posts

Every second of this embodiment from now on can be spent in transcendent service to mankind. You do not

have to preach. You do not have to stand forth to
perform a miracle. All you have to do is to *live* the Law,
and live it so beautifully that you cause others to do
likewise.

For every unselfish, beautiful thing that you do, I
pour forth My Love in an unending stream to you; but
when you persist in wasting your energy in turning your
attention upon things of little moment, when you persist
in arguing, when you persist in seeing the false in one
another, I cannot help you, for I help the one most who
feels himself nearest to Me, who loves Me greatest and
wants My assistance sufficiently to recognize My qualities
in himself.

Whether or not you know that I am real, still do you
know that these words are real. Then give heed and
learn how to silence your human self. Learn to pour forth
a constant stream of love to all things. Learn to live in
harmony and peace with one another. Then will all those
who come within your radiant embrace accept the Light
through your love, and stand with you to bring in the
New Golden Age.

You do not need a manifestation before you to show
you that these Laws are true. You yourself are the great
manifestation and these great magnificent truths are your
guide posts which take you along the road of life. When
you have thus safely come onto this great road, this
Mighty Highway that leads you into the Eternal Realms
of Light, when the guide posts are there marking your
way clearly, why will you any longer permit your
attention to be held by outer conditions? Banish them
from your world as you would a poisonous serpent and
turn your attention to your Presence and accept only
that blessing entering into your heart, filling your world
with Light. Refuse acceptance of all human things or
human limitations. Accept your complete mastery of
your physical body, of your mental body. Command all
to come into Divine Order through the Power of Divine
Love pouring forth from your heart.

Those things which you have determined upon to do, do them perfectly. Inasmuch as you understand yourself to be a part of God, you must see that God will not be employed upon a trivial matter. Accept your responsibility as a God Being. You will never advance very far unless you accept your responsibility. Additional responsibility accepted in wisdom always brings an expansion of Light in the world of the individual accepting the responsibility.

Do not attempt to escape your responsibilities as a creator for you have been brought forth the image and likeness of Almighty God. You are endowed by the Creator with the Power of the Creator, and each one has the Power of Creation, the Power of Manifestation, the Power of Precipitation. You can no more help creating than you can help living, for you are Life, and your Life is the power of Creation. Think upon these things and then apply yourselves as never before. Do not hang back waiting for that last opportunity to open up, but drive forward, calling to your I AM Presence.

The Great Law of Life, the Great Law of Justice and Balance that governs immutably throughout the Earth has decreed that each individual must stand squarely on his own feet and face the Great Blazing, Dazzling Light of his own Presence, Conquering all.

Remember: We are speaking of the Laws of Life, not religious doctrine!

IV

THE FIRE OF CREATION
by Saint Germain.

I wish you to understand that first and foremost this Law which I have brought forth to mankind, which is exactly the same Law as it was thousands of years ago and will always be the same, this Law is practical, and if applied in a practical way will bring practical results. The important thing to remember always, of course, is your I AM Presence and Its location in reference to your physical body, as well as the doorway to your Presence, which is within your heart. Having this before your consciousness and with your attention focused upon the highest possible ideals, you will undoubtedly, as an individual, be rendering a great service in a very practical way, and that, My dear children, is the way this Law is to be given to mankind.

I assure you that these laws, which are so real and so practical, have been released to the children of Earth for the specific purpose of raising their vibratory action and their consciousness to make them worthy of the new civilization, which is even now unfolding before them.

My activity has nothing to do with religion, but it has a great deal to do with the spiritual understanding of mankind, since it is the full Law in that regard. How practical this Law is to you will, of course, depend upon your application, but I assure you that the imperative thing, aside from the single fact of keeping your consciousness upon your own Presence, is the maintaining of the highest possible ideals, and there is no exception to that!

If your attention and your desire constantly focus upon ideals that are less than perfect, then with your knowledge of the Law they will come to pass much more rapidly than they would if you did not have this understanding. Therefore, once knowing the Law, it is absolutely imperative that you learn constantly to focus your attention upon the very highest possible, which is, of course, perfection. You must indeed be Master, for ye are indeed the children of God.

In bringing you this Law of Life, it has been My endeavor not to tell you of Myself, but rather of the Great Law; not to turn your attention nor mankind's attention personally to those who carried My message, but rather to the Message itself, that humanity might at last recognize its own God Presence, the I AM, and abide in that Great Wondrous All-enfolding Light of God That Never Fails.

There is nothing more important, there is no single thing of greater magnitude than the stilling of oneself and the knowing, the conscious acceptance of the fact that the I AM Presence is within you, is your individualized source of God in action. That is the supreme knowledge which has been released. The Glory of God is very real.

Blessed ones, the law of energy and vibration is such that at least three-fourths of your energy, the energy acting in your world, remains to act in the feeling body. You will very quickly see that as you call the Presence into action—that is when your feelings are not disturbed—and ask that the energy in your feeling world be held calm and at peace, you will have, as the momentum is gained, established a marvelous means of protecting yourself against all disturbing conditions.

Now a little less than one-fourth of the energy which is acting in your world operates through the mental body. I am not referring now to the Higher Mental Body, but to the mental body, the point of sense consciousness in the individual's thought world. The remainder of the energy, which is a small portion indeed, operates in the other bodies, such as the etheric, etc. Thus you will see very quickly that if you as an individual will do as suggested, and call the Presence into action to harmonize the feeling world and keep it harmonized, you will begin to establish for yourself a mighty momentum of calm, peace, and serenity which will very swiftly become so powerful that no human disturbing thing can get you off balance, even for an instant.

When your feelings are already upset and the accumulation of energy in your feeling world is being released in a destructive or discordant way, there is one thing which you can do which will positively assist you in regaining the control which you may have temporarily lost—that is to get away from the condition which is confronting you at the moment, get yourself still, and then turn your attention to your mental world and ask for the illumination which will assist you in perceiving the truth of the situation which has temporarily disturbed you. Then as the illumination comes to you from the I AM Presence you will begin to see the reason behind the activity and, when that point occurs and your feelings begin to be harmonized, do not hesitate, but go directly again to the place where the condition has caused the disturbance and there take your conquering stand. There is the place to call your Presence into action to release Its Full Power to control your feelings, to harmonize them, that never again will that appearance which has caused the temporary disturbance have power to act in your world.

One of the things which humanity does not seem to comprehend is that unless the individual will definitely make application to still his feelings and harmonize them and use the determination of the I AM Presence acting through his mental world, he positively will be the prey to his own feelings, and those feelings, once they have been energized and released into action will continue to act sometimes for days after the incident that has caused the action has been completely forgotten. And as that energy is three times as much as you find in the mental world is the reason why so many times you will be feeling fine, that is, your mind will be clear although unknown to you there may be something acting in your feeling world of which you are not aware, and all of a sudden something will drive in to upset you, or an accident will take place, which is caused only because of the disturbing feeling which may have occurred two or three days before it acted in your world.

You see how absolutely imperative it is for you to learn to be master of all thoughts and feelings. *You cannot rise into the Arisen Master's octave until you have learned to govern your attention, your power of qualification, and your vision,* for those are the three God attributes which every human being has, and there is no human being who can say: "Well, some other has greater attributes in this direction than I—or—I am not able to apply this as I should because so and so." Those things are positively not true! Every individual in calling his I AM Presence into action, becomes supreme over his world, and there is no human being who can interfere long if he is sincere and makes his application.

We find so often blessed ones will learn of these great Laws, begin making their application and realize there is tremendous power in connection with them, and they will go on expecting miracles. Very soon their very expectancy will turn sour because their attention is on the miracle and they will say: "It doesn't work. I have tried it for six years, or sixty." Well, dear ones, please remember that this great Law which has been brought to you is the fulfilling Law of Life itself and there is no short cut. You yourself must go every step of the way by yourself, remember that! You cannot go it with another, nor can you go it by another's effort. You yourself must make the application. Your feeling world is vast and will positively control you unless you, in your calls to the Presence, build a momentum which permits the illumination of the I AM Presence to flood forth through you to act as a clearing force so that you are instantly above it.

You will find that the individuals in the world today who are causing such great destruction are those who have not learned to use the Light from the Presence but rather are using the emotion from the feeling world. That is the reason that individuals have the power temporarily to cause destruction, for without waiting for the Light of God to illumine their minds that they may have understanding and balance, they release tremendous vicious energy through upset feelings, and that energy acts and has tremendous power.

Since feeling contains the greatest percentage of your energy, of course it is the quickest thing to get out of control, and once it sweeps out of control, the attention, in fact, the entire activity of the mind is very quick to follow. The mind, on the other hand, should that get out of control, the feeling, if harmonious, would bring it into order; therefore, you see that it is absolutely imperative that you govern your feelings. Make no mistake about that! Governing and controlling the feelings does not mean you cease to have feelings, but it does means that you learn to govern them with iron control.

Consider the various forces which play upon the feeling world and through the mental world. Remember always, you are dealing with force, therefore, you will quickly see that you must always be tolerant of the individual, for the very force which may play through you at one moment, will, while playing through you upset some individual, and the next moment play through the individual and upset you. Few realize this, for when a force is operating through you, you are not aware of it, you are only aware of it as it begins to affect those about you. Think about that. Usually these various forces which man has generated will play through one or another and that one be unaware that it is taking place, whereas others will have no reaction; but should they begin to criticize or condemn they open themselves to the same force and become a channel for it, to the dismay of those who are not as yet under its influence.

When individuals' feeling worlds become upset they go on and on in an upset state until either they call on the Fire of Forgiveness or they build a great form, which in turn acts and continues to act until a shock takes place severe enough to jar them loose from that which they have created. That is why we see man today suffering from such a vast accumulation of misqualified feeling, and that is why we see the things taking place that are taking place, for it takes a shock to break yourself loose from your own human creation. And when you have once been shaken loose from it you have the opportunity and the power to clear your world of your human creation, which is not possible as long as you are connected with it. But what a blessing to know that when you call your own I AM Presence into action you take a permanent step toward your own Victory, whereas when you, through some lack of application or mistaken idea, create some form which is not perfect, it has no permanent place and does not act as a permanent hindrance to you. Your I AM Presence takes you forward and there is no going back. How man should rejoice in the Power of Light that beats his heart!

Just as long as periodically you permit your feelings to become disturbed because of the action of some individual, just so long you will never advance beyond a certain stage. You must maintain harmony within your feelings whether dealing with magnificent individuals who understand their own God Presence, or dealing with what we could almost call human rats, it makes no difference.

You must be above all desire to take authority. You

must be above all desire to take offense, for you must always have enough respect for yourself to recognize the God Flame acting within you; and when you acknowledge that, and are at-one with your own God Presence, the Great I AM, you will have no reason ever for losing control over your feelings.

If We were to talk about this thing for the next ten years We could not talk about it enough. *You must learn to control your feelings*. It is imperative! You cannot go beyond a certain point until you have done so. That is what is the matter with the majority of the people upon this planet. They are constantly flaring up because of little insignificant things, and because of that, the feeling grows. Remember, Light and Energy are one. Light and Energy everywhere present is God in Action, and you cannot release energy misqualified and not expect to receive the return force acting upon you.

Seek to govern your outer self. The only thing that stands between yourself and instantaneous manifestation is your human self which doubts the activity of God. When you make a call, if you do not receive the answer as quickly as you think you should, know the obstacle must be in your human self, for there is no obstacle to God. When you have loved enough you may command the universe and it will bow and create at your behest.

Control your feelings no matter what may be revealed to you. This is the schoolroom where you learn mastery—where you learn never to be surprised or off guard—never to be disappointed and never to be too elated, especially at your own progress; where you learn to be humble in all things; to be gracious, kind, beautiful, and harmonious. This is the schoolroom of Life where you learn the *Rules of Life*. Whatever you may learn, wherever you may go, whatever you may do, stand guard over your feelings, stand guard over your attention, and pour forth Love and Gratitude at all times.

Blessed ones, will you not see that you must take a more positive stand in that you must understand these laws and abide in them. Let your feeling pour forth, under control, of course, but with great determination. Your feeling, dear ones, is your life, for as a man thinketh in his heart so is he, and as a man thinketh in his heart so does he feel. Your feeling is that great reservoir of energy which is where the greatest portion of your consciousness remains, and if that consciousness is alive and filled with Light and action, you yourself are filled with Light and action, but if you refuse to send forth a feeling of love, through fear that you will send forth a misqualified feeling, you go through the activity of stifling yourself until something some place has to give way. Release your love in an unending stream in gratitude to Life and to your fellow man for all those things which have come to you.

Determine that you will from this time on be absolutely calm and controlled in your feelings, and while you are calm pour forth your dynamic, positive love and blessings to everyone. Know, and make no mistake about it, when you accept the Arisen Masters' Ideals of Life you stand with Us. When you determine to follow the path which takes you to those Ideals you walk beside Us. However, when you accept the Full Glory of your Presence in your heart you rise among Us.

Do not be concerned about the activity of human beings. Just know that the I AM Presence is the Only Power in the Universe and before It all things must come into order. There is no reason or excuse at any time to allow little feelings of doubt to drive into your world. Silence them and go forward into Victory! Learn to control your spoken words and your actions! Avoid the appearance of evil! Be true to the Light within you and you will find the Light will protect its own, and you will walk through unharmed when destruction is about you.

It is your obligation as students not only to apply these laws but to call them into action to release an activity of feeling to stem the tide of the destructive force. That is the activity of energy directed by intelligence—not your intelligence but the Intelligence of the I AM Presence flowing through you. That is not emotional, nor intended to be emotional, but it is something that does require feelings under control.

You will see very quickly that unless you as individuals will make your application with feeling you can accomplish little. Just a mental call is not sufficient and you will never overcome the destructive energy released by humanity by just thinking your way through You will have to take a strong, positive stand and release a strong flow of energy. Be perfectly balanced and at ease at all times. But the release of energy alone is not sufficient, for that energy must be directed with Intelligence, with Courage, with Love; for just the release of energy will add to the disturbing condition in the world. What is required so definitely is the release of energy with the power of the White Light of the Presence, the pure white Intelligence of the Great I AM, directed so that it flows to its goal to perform its perfect work.

Remember that you are beings of Love; remember that you are beings of Joy; remember that you are beings of Victory! Your love, your joy, and your victory will come about when you put your I AM Presence *first* and everything else second. The unfortunate thing which chains individuals to limitation is that instead of putting God, the I AM Presence first, they persist in putting some human being first, or some human desire first, or some human occupation first, and just so long as there is a false God in the way of love to the Presence and the attention to the Presence, just so long will that individual be unable to control his thoughts and feelings—will be unable to gain his own mastery. You may be sure of that.

Feeling World—Emotional World

One is the activity of the human—the other is the activity of the Divine.

The feeling world is the world whose center is the heart and from which flows the feeling of Love, of Happiness, of Generosity, and all the Arisen Master qualities which operate at the level of the heart.

The emotional world is the world whose center is the solar plexus, and from it pour forth the emotions of hate, anger, jealousy, criticism, and the qualities which are far from the Arisen Master octave—in other words, the opposite.

Thus you will see that the two, while both capable of releasing the same type of energy, are as far apart as the poles, for one is human and the other is Divine.

As you assist in controlling your own feeling world you assist in the expansion of the Light.

Feelings—The Fire Of Creation

The Fire of Creation, the Fire of Life itself is held within the feelings and every feeling which you release is Fire. If the feeling is one which is governed by Love and by the desire to bless, the action is beneficent, beautiful, wholly pure and perfect, and you have the activity of the pure Flame of Life. This Flame may take on any quality which the individual sends forth in his feeling; that is, if it is a feeling of Love, the flame will doubtless be pink with a slight touch of gold; if the feeling be Wisdom, the gold will predominate; if the quality be Peace or Generosity, it will be green, and if purifying, the fire will be violet., etc. If the individual does not care to qualify the feeling but sends forth instead a feeling of deep devotion to the Presence, asking that the Presence release the feeling, the flame will be almost pure white tinged with a little blue. If the individual sends forth a destructive feeling the element of fire is still present; however, instead of being a flame, the feeling world releases lightning, the jagged barbs of which penetrate and tear the substance of the feeling world, not only of the individual who sends it forth but of the individual to whom it is directed. This is

painful in the extreme, as many know. The feeling world
corresponds to the element of fire.

Seven Stages Of Consciousness

1st: In the beginning, the ego released into embodiment
after he has turned away from the Presence and sought
new things, becomes first of all a creature of emotional
desire. He lives only to satisfy his own selfish desires. He
has no thought of love or concern for another; his entire
action is the fulfilling of his own selfish appetites. He will
do a great deal of eating, a great deal of wasting of
energy, will very rarely have any kind of thought that
would take him into a higher realm of action than his
own stomach, and for the most part will not remain very
long in physical embodiment. That is the first action of
the developing consciousness from the human standpoint.

2nd: In the next action we find the individual becoming
aware of the rights of others, not to the extent that he is
able to assist others in obtaining those rights, but he
becomes conscious of group action and group activity,
and because the progress is still quite slow in his own
desires to satisfy himself, to fill his own stomach, to give
way to every conceivable emotion and sense gratification,
he usually falls into the activity of desiring to exercise
power over his fellows. He is a step ahead of those in the
first plane of consciousness because he is aware of others
and aware of their desires, even though he desires to
master them and make all others subservient to himself.
Now strange as it seems to you, there are a vast number
of individuals in embodiment today who still, regardless
of the appearance of their bodies, belong to these first
two classes.

3rd: Then we move out of the classification of those
who not only understand the desires of others, at least to
some extent, but have accepted in a measure the

obligation to live and let live. The desire to have power over their fellows is no longer of paramount importance but rather there is a desire to be let alone so that they can indulge in their own sense gratification and also the desire to see to it that the others have the same opportunity for sense enjoyment. Now this is the third level of consciousness, in which the great mass of humanity finds itself today.

4th: Then as we move out of that level of consciousness into the fourth activity we find the student really entering upon the pathway of Light consciousness. These other planes of consciousness are the levels which, although upon the pathway, are never consciously there. This is the place where the individual accepts that there is something more to life than the satisfying of his own personal desires. Still, the personal desires have a great controlling power over the individual's life but he is beginning to look higher than that. This is the fourth plane of consciousness.

5th: Now in the fifth plane of consciousness the individual has learned that there is a great power, although invisible to him for the most part, which can and will bring order everywhere it moves. The individual at this level is often very confused because he has not quite as yet adjusted himself to the clearing of his own world from his own desires and the replacing of them in his world with God desires. This is a very trying period for each one to pass through, but entering into the sixth realm is where the individual ceases to live for self and lives only to be of service to others.

6th: In the sixth realm the individual has conquered all desire to profit personally, no longer has desires for sense gratification, and is living only for the purpose of assisting others.

7th: From there we move into the seventh and final pre-

paratory stage for the ascension. In this stage the individual has become sufficiently master of his own world
to be upon the conscious pathway at all times. He has
already learned how to contact those Beings Who are
Arisen and is sufficiently in control of himself to be
above every temptation of every sort. The ascension is
very near to him.

Now these various gradations are, of course, broken
down into many, many degrees of advancement, but it is
not our intention to go into that matter now. There are
some whom you will observe belong even as high as the
sixth plane, where they are rendering a great service to
others, and yet in some action of the consciousness have
never really passed even the first or second state of
consciousness, because the individual in advancing will go
very rapidly in one direction and very slowly in another,
so it would be very difficult to tell where the individual
stands. However, with study, you as an individual can
determine at what level of consciousness you stand.

V

STAIRWAY TO MASTERY

by various Masters.

Call to your God Presence and accept that great Light and the constant promptings as they come. If you do not succeed the first time, do not become discouraged. Seek to govern your outer self.

As you use the activity of the I AM Presence you gain a powerful momentum, for each call that you make releases a current of energy which forms a pattern. This same pattern becomes more and more positive, more and more powerful with the number of calls made. Thus you will see that to attain Mastery you must practice Perfection. Learn to still yourself and then, recognizing that Blazing Light of the I AM, turn to it and accept its Full Power, even in little things.

Train yourself always to be alert and on guard—alert that you may never miss an opportunity to pour forth Love and Blessings—on guard that you will always watch your own feeling world and never permit yourself even in jest to pour forth a negative thought or feeling. Do not mistake the activity of standing guard or being alert with a critical attitude which watches for mistakes of others.

Your concern is always with yourself. Make your own intense application and you will be free.

You have noticed so many times how today you will be up and very joyous and tomorrow you will feel very down and everything going the wrong way. Now if you will call to the Great Host of Light you will find Their Consciousness will assist in sustaining a Joyous, Victorious feeling within you. Just your calls to the I AM Presence are not enough, for if you want the sustained activity you must have the permanency which only the Arisen Masters can give. Sincere application on this will bring great victory and release to you.

When you make a call in the name of your great Presence of Life, I AM, recognize your authority! Think of what you are saying! Feel the reality of what you are saying! Accept it! And in that thinking, feeling and acceptance you will have the fulfillment which will come to you so rapidly you hardly think it possible.

Know always that in your calls to God, the great, magnificent, Wondrous Presence of Life, I AM, which is within your heart, which is anchored above you in that Great Blazing Sun of Light, that in your calls to that Source, there is no power that can interfere with the fulfillment of those calls.

Know definitely, now and for all time, that when you make a call in the name of Life, in the name of your own great Presence of Life, I AM, when you make that call you have set into motion the Immutable Laws of the Universe which sweep into action, and no force, human opinion or condition can turn aside that decree until it is fulfilled. Never look to the answer, look only to the Presence, and accept in your calls the Fullness of Life's answer to you.

When you call in the Name of God, in the Name of I AM, there is no power in heaven or on earth that can say to that call "stand aside." That call goes forth. It will not be denied, and the fulfillment of that call is inevitable! Now watch that you do not be dismayed at the result when you make that call. Stand firm and steadfast, with joy in your heart, knowing that as you make the call you have fulfilled your destiny, you have fulfilled the Great Cosmic Command concerning Light!

The Conquering Presence recognizes Perfection and commands it to fill Infinity. You, in your calls to that Great Presence of Life, which you are, can command that perfection to flow into your world and into the world of anyone else wherever your attention may turn. If you see a condition that is less than perfection you don't have to shut your eyes to it, you don't have to ignore it, but you do have to stand fast and command perfection to manifest there, and you have the authority to do so!

Remember always that regardless of all of the Law of Life and its explanation that has been given, it has been given by the Masters to achieve your Victory, and you must take your own responsibility and make your own mighty application.

Always call first to your own God Presence, and then when that call is completed you may call to the Masters, who will be happy to assist. Progress must come through the individual. Even the Arisen Masters cannot do that for you. If you look to the Master to do these things for you, then He must withdraw His radiation. You cannot lean on Him. Each one alone must face his Mighty God Presence, his own lifestream. The fundamentals of the Laws of Life are the foundations on which you build mansions. This is the way you move onward to the higher consciousness; but never do the mansions take the place of the foundation. That foundation—I AM—is the Principle of Life. The student must come to know that. What mankind needs is Love, the understanding of Love.

Know that in your call to the Presence, the Great I AM, you give to your Presence your own life, all those things which you have and are. Do not fall into the outer world habits. Dare to go into the Father's House and stand alone facing the Sunlight within. Say often:

"I AM the Power of Divine Love filling the hearts and minds of mankind everywhere and releasing to them the Sustaining Power of Life in Action in their beings and worlds."

If you want rapid manifestation, never cease to call for the blessing of another. Command in the Name of Life for these things. Do not dwell on things of the outer world. Perfection must come forth in the physical octave, but it comes by the power of attention to the higher octaves. Never forget to make the call for the rest of mankind, for only then will the floodgates open wide and the Mighty River of your own Life flow forth to bring you every perfect thing.

Banish all doubt and fear. They are the things that stand in your way. Do not have any concern over another, excepting that you may be of service. Know always that the Power of Light is real and knows no opposite. Affirm: "I AM the Full Power of Light in Action filling my mind, my being, my world, then flooding forth into the world of all mankind; for I AM the Action of Life, I AM the Presence of Life, I AM the Victory of Life now and forever!"

In making your calls to the I AM Presence and the Arisen Masters, be sincere! Mean what you say! It is far better for you to make one really sincere, determined call than to make fifty half-hearted attempts. One call released with a positive feeling, with sincerity, with love, will do more good, waste less time, bring about more happiness than all the half-hearted attempts in the world!

Never tire of making your application, but it must be made correctly. Let us have no more of this calling to the Presence to destroy! Never intrude upon an individual's free will. An individual who calls to the I AM Presence to destroy another individual or to bring discord into his world, or to do something destructive or negative—an individual who makes such a call is using black magic! Regardless of the amount of application which you have made, unless you have been willing to apply your learning of these laws from a practical standpoint there is much which you probably do not fully comprehend.

It is a very easy matter to sit still, to study these Great Laws and to visualize how magnificent the perfection will be when it comes about. It is a far more difficult matter to set about bringing them into fulfillment but that is the course which must be pursued. Put aside thoughts of self. What matter where some one stands, of what matter what some one says! There is only one thing that matters and that is more Light—greater and greater Light poured forth. Think upon that!

You have to make your own effort, dear ones. You have to apply these Laws by yourself, no one can apply them for you. Then rejoice, for your rejoicing itself is part of the Law, and recognizing that oneness, the oneness between yourself and your own Divinity, the Magic Presence; the oneness between yourself and other human beings; the Oneness between yourself and the Great Cosmic Space where you all are One. Accept that, feel that oneness, and then claim your God Authority, command God Perfection for yourself and for every part of you.

You can call to your I AM Presence to give you limitless ideas, more and more perfection constantly, so why not do it? Do not wait for some one to put you to work. There is no one who has ever been put in authority over your lifestream. You are your own authority. Then take that authority and have the Glory and the Joy that comes in calling to your own I AM Presence that Its qualities be permitted to flow through you unmolested. You must see that these things which you desire and the Perfection which you wish to bring forth must come forth as a result of your own application, your own God picture of Perfection.

Never tire of calling to the I AM Presence. That Presence is the Great Reality, the Pure Christ Light which fills your veins, your nerves, every fiber of your being and the atmosphere around you with Light and Love. Turn to that Great and Mighty Presence, blessed ones, and by turning to It I do not merely mean to turn to it quickly, although that is very helpful too in an emergency, but I mean turn to It in reverence, in love, and worship, that you may have Its power pouring through your world to assist you and bless you. Accept the responsibility of the mighty channel that you are becoming, each of you, and never let any individual interfere with your progress in that direction.

Know that there is no hiding thoughts, motives, subtle human desires, all of those things which you do not wish to have anyway, and which can never be hidden from your own God-self, the Great I AM. What a great sense of Joy and Happiness, of Freedom, comes to one when he realizes that he does not have to hide anything, because he cannot do so anyway. Then he knows that Truth, Honesty, Openness are the only qualities; and knowing that, the Light blazes forth in all its Glory.

Never apply to the point where you are exhausted, or your mind ceases to function, or you do not feel yourself master of what you are doing. When you get to that point it is the indication that you have overstepped the bounds and you should get back into a calm, serene way of doing things.

If, in your earnest determination to bring forth some particular manifestation you become too dynamic, too determined, you many times repel that which the Presence already has in store for you. You see the I AM Presence is the Presence that beats your heart and that Presence does not need to be shouted at, it does not even need to be told twice. It knows in advance what you require, what you shall do, for of course, your Perfect Plan, your Perfect Pattern is within It. How simple it is to see then that your application to your Presence can be very dynamic or it can be very peaceful, yet the place where the dynamic energy must be released is from the human standpoint, for the human often rebels and it is necessary to take a very strong stand when one is confronted with one's own activity.

In calling to the Presence, do not feel that physical effort is needed. Feel rather that sincerity is the human requirement. You do not have to wave your arms around to contact your Presence. You must enter into the silence, into the heart of your Presence, and there feel the Full Power of that Light which is the Great I AM within you and accept Its mighty radiation, Its mighty Power of Light pouring through you. That is a perfectly natural activity and will always be beneficial. You may be absolutely certain that nothing discordant, inharmonious or negative ever in any way comes from the Presence of God; therefore, have no fear in calling the Presence into action and asking for Its dominion in your world and in the world and affairs of your Nation.

For many years now the Arisen Masters have given to mankind of Earth the understanding whereby they can free themselves from their own human creation and desires which would rend and tear and divide, yet unless you will apply that understanding you cannot be free. You, yourself, of your own volition must make the application, and whereas there have been some who have made tremendous progress and application, there have been others who have just lain by the wayside for some miracle to take place or somebody to do something for them, until they have actually stopped making progress, and that is a very serious situation in this cosmic period in which we live.

Humanity upon this planet is facing its most serious lesson, for until the Law of Love governs humanity, mankind will be governed by its own human passions, its own human desires. You as a member of the great body of humanity must make your choice, but it is important that you understand that just because there are human things acting in the great mass of mankind, this does not in any way excuse those forces acting in you. Understand that! That has been the activity of the human consciousness for thousands of years. Individuals have said: "Well, if that person couldn't be perfect, then neither can I," and that is exactly the thing which has caused the downfall of so many blessed ones.

You must take your positive stand that regardless of all humanity, you yourself will stand absolutely Pure and Perfect and will not accept any human condition! You have to take that stand yourself, and there is no human personality, human condition, or human power that can deprive you of your Victory if you take that stand. And when you yourself take that stand I will stand by your side and take you by the hand in such a tangible way that you will know the great reality which I AM.

Do not misunderstand this, as so many of those who seek the pathway seem to misunderstand. You must make your decrees so your human form stands aside to let the God Power flow forth. This does not mean the entire activity of the day should be given over to decrees or application, nor that after making the application you are entirely free of responsibility so that you release and forget what must be accomplished. Remember, blessed ones, it is the Power of God released working through you that accomplishes the great miracles; and miracles have been wrought and are being wrought today by some not consciously on the pathway, and others on the pathway. The Laws given by the Arisen Masters are not laws to permit you to escape from the reality of life, but to master life, and since the only enemy you have is you, know your application is directed so that the human self will become the God-self in the Oneness of All Things. Then you take your Scepter of Authority and command in the Master's Name and it will be done.

Remember, dear ones, it is not the human that does the raising; it is the Power of Light released in your calls, in your own acceptance of that Power of Light as it floods forth. Do not, I beg of you, make the call and then turn around looking for the result. Accept that there is neither time nor space, for they have been set aside.

Accept that even as you make the call, the answer is here. Do not feel any sense of strain. Remember, dear hearts, your responsibility ends as you place it in God's Hands. Call the I AM Presence into action and know that in so doing you have fulfilled the Law; and the power of that call and the acceptance of the result is all that is required for perfection to manifest.

The situation which you find in the world today having to do with those seeking to hold the Light is extremely hazardous, a situation augmented frequently by the unconcern, the lassitude or laziness of those who really are informed but who seem to think in some way all things will come right and they have to make no effort to secure that rightness. You must know now and for all time that those things which are to be accomplished are accomplished only with the release of energy. You are the source, you in physical bodies, from which the call and the energy must be released. Only with your cooperation and participation can the Fullness of the Light be released to you. Never let down in your application, and know that in your heart you are the Victorious Presence at all times.

I wish you to understand unmistakably, those of you who are comparatively new to this work, that you cannot enter into the Fullness of your Great I AM Presence without application. Know that as easy as these truths may seem to you, you do not rise into your perfection by seemingly refusing to do negative things. *You must make positive application!* This does not mean you must practice abstinence or privation, but you must be determined you are going to accomplish, through self-discipline and correction, if you wish to attain your Freedom and Eternal Victory. There are some who feel that through the natural process of living they will, over a period of many embodiments, be raised into their perfection and they do not have to make any effort to attain this; but if that were true everyone would have made his ascension a long time ago.

It is that very feeling of nonconcern, that lack-
adaisical way of looking at life, which causes man to
drift and tie himself on the wheel of birth and rebirth.
You cannot be half way in and half way out of your
service to the Light. You either are going to serve the
Light or you are not, and you must make up your mind
irrevocably. If you serve the Light then there are certain
things to put aside, and you will have to determine what
is to be put aside and make your application for that to
happen. You are master of your world, no one else. What
you say and think and feel, you decree into your world.
If you maintain the thought or feeling in your
consciousness that you can continue on with certain
human habits and still go forward raising yourself into
greater and greater perfection, you are only deluding
yourself. *You must make the application!* This does not mean
you must be stiff and tense, but you must be
sincere in your effort, and you must make the effort!
You must apply and again apply! There is no power in
heaven or earth that can stop the onrushing expansion of
Light when you call the Presence into action. But if you
will not call It into action and follow the old mental
process of figuring out the action, you will not
accomplish anything more than anybody else.

It may seem hard for some of you to apply, and also,
it may seem that the outer world interferes, but if you
believe in the Light, if you value that little Flame of God
in your heart, if you believe in the Arisen Host of Light,
if you believe in yourself, you will make a supreme effort
to stop the silly nonsense of saying that the outer world
is taking up all of your time, and you will find time to
make the application necessary to draw about you the
Wall of Protection, to draw in and through you the Power
of this Light.

Say as you work, as you move about, as you walk
down the street—"I AM harmonious." There is not one
of you who cannot apply that as you do whatever you
are doing. Even those who have to mentally concentrate,

there are thousands of seconds which tick in between that mental work, which can be put to use by constructive thought and feeling. You are thinking all the time, and if you will investigate carefully and run off a little record of your thoughts you will find how many of them are petty worries. Those petty worries are human, and unnecessary thought and feeling going forth. It is filling your world with rubbish. Instead, if you have a little worry or a big worry, a small problem or a large problem, say: "I AM the Presence pouring into this condition, solving it for me right now." Then—"I AM harmonious, I AM Peaceful. I AM alert to the direction of my God-self as it flows through me," etc., etc. There are thousands of statements which you can use that will correct these little worries and bring about correct creation through your form.

You must create constructive thoughts and feelings! You must become finished with worries and wonderings, and questionings of the kind that—"I wonder this, and I wonder that—should I? shouldn't I?" and so on. Be firm with yourself, and remember, as you make your application, as you make your calls, such as: "I AM Light, and I Am Harmonious," etc., remember to do them with *feeling* and *vision* in your Heart. Visualize a flowing of Light from your Heart, and when you make that statement visualize that particular thing. If you say: "I Am Perfect," then see the Light in your Heart flow forth, acknowledge it, and then as you pour that forth out through you, accept the Perfection. It will take hold and act. O you may not see it transpire just the very next second because you have a big work to do to raise that form, but just know it must act when you precede these statements with "I Am." When you precede statements with "I Am," this Great Action is a creative thing and it creates. It is a thought and feeling that goes into action. It opens the floodgates through your form creating an outflow of your Presence, and that goes through you and causes your own self to rise and expand.

Stand at-one with that great Presence regardless of
any human appearance, comment, or condition! Stand
at-one with that Presence and know unmistakably that in
that Light which is the Presence you cannot fail! Never
tire in your earnest application; but remember to keep
your progress to yourself. Make your application! Know
you are at-one with your own Infinite I AM Self, and
abide in that Sacred, Beautiful Place, accepting nothing
but the Power of God which flows forth to fill your
being, every atom, your consciousness, and your physical
body with more and ever more of Itself.

Dear ones, never tire of turning to that great,
Glorious, Golden Light of God, the I AM Presence that
beats your heart, that thrills you right down to your
finger tips, to every fiber of your being, and makes you
aware of your oneness with the Limitless Power of the
Universe. So often sincere students, because there is no
particular manifestation, because there is no great,
exciting thing taking place, periodically become discouraged, and since they do not see a manifestation of something startling, a miracle of sorts taking place before their
eyes, they become discouraged, their calls weaken in
effect and in frequency, and after a while they just drift
along and hope.

Blessed ones, know always that in your achievement
of Victory, as you call the Presence into action you have
passed the hoping consciousness, you have arrived at the
Commanding Consciousness of the most powerful and
most potent force of Life throughout the universe. You,
as you stand at-one with your Presence, Command the
entire Universe with Authority! Never forget that! Even
though, physically speaking, you may be very humble,
very ordinary (you may think), still in your call to the
Presence and in your acceptance of that Great Light
which you are, you have become at-one with the Great
Immutable Forces that rule all things created and
uncreated. Never tire of that, and recognize that as you
make your progress you are rapidly rising and ever rising

into the Arisen State, where you rightfully belong. Isn't it wonderful to know these marvelous things which await you and the progress you make as you call your Presence into action?

Be sincere in the release of the Light that you call forth. You know, if you would spend half the energy in calling your Presence into action that you sometimes spend wondering where you can get more information about the Presence, you would know more about the Presence, because you would be closer to it. What you must realize is that the Victory of your own lifestream is in your own keeping. But how else would you have it if you were planning the universe? Isn't it glorious to know that you stand at-one with this great Light that Never Fails!

Blessed ones, you have not made a call by just abstractly thinking of your Presence. You must actually go through the mental and feeling process of making the call, releasing the words silently or in the spoken word. That is one of the steps, but it alone is not sufficient. You must not only release the words through your mind and voice, but you must also release the feeling of what you are doing. Turn your attention to your Presence, recognize that Presence as the only power that can act in your world, call it into action with determination, with feeling. If you wish to learn more of these laws, dear ones, turn to that Presence and ask for the release of additional understanding, and feel as you ask that you really desire to know, and that which you desire, that which you require will be given to you.

You cannot rise into the Perfected State without making your application. It is all a matter of energy. You must call that Mighty Law into action, for you are the commander and the decreer of what will be done in your world. You have within yourself the right and the authority to command Perfection for your world, and there isn't anyone else who can command it for you. The

Elder Brothers have said that if it could have been done,
They would have done it for you long ago.

So many times Beloved Jesus has longed to do that
very thing, and so many of the outer and orthodox
churches have fallen into the erroneous conclusion that
He did that very thing, that because of His great
experience and service to mankind two thousand years
ago, that humanity has been saved. Well, of course, in
actual fact, humanity has not been lost, but humanity is
insisting on trying to lose itself. Humanity refuses to
recognize that each individual must make the necessary
application to rise up out of imperfection. An example is
only an example. Man must walk this pathway himself.
The Great Eternal Fiat of Creation is *Be ye perfect*! and
you cannot be perfect and continue to have imperfect
thoughts and feelings in your mind and in your world.
Turn to that Great Presence, the Mighty Blazing Light
which you are, and seek for guidance and understanding.
Discipline yourself! Love and happiness is the pathway,
the joyous pathway strewn with roses.

It is no longer necessary for you to torture yourselves
in order to achieve perfection. You do not have to whip
yourselves, deny yourselves, curtail yourselves, repress
yourselves—that is not necessary—although some years
ago it was very nearly imperative in view of the darkness
and degradation of the mental emanations of mankind;
but today it is possible for the sincere student to grasp
the Scepter of Dominion and put aside thoughts of greed,
envy, avarice, lust, etc. It is possible for you as students
to become the Living Emblem of Love itself. Then why
not make the application? At this level of consciousness
where man stands he is never free. He is caught on the
wheel that turns slowly, inexorably on, but in your calls
to your Presence you remove yourself from the necessity
of the recurring pattern of cause and effect and rise into
the Realm of Cause alone.

You must learn to rely fully on your own God-self,
recognizing that all-powerful, all-pervading Presence in

everything that you do, everywhere that you go, accepting that Presence as the only Power that can act, not only in your world but in the world of everyone with whom you come in contact, and it is wise to remind yourself of this activity at all times. If you will only train yourself to call that I AM Presence into action over the little things, you will very quickly have gained a momentum which will bring you every big thing.

Tremendous energy is wasted in doubting thoughts and feelings, in thinking human things. Were that same energy applied in turning to the Presence, asking for guidance, man's world would be beautiful and everything would begin coming into Divine Order. Dear ones, it takes no more energy to think of the Law than it takes to criticize and condemn another. Charge yourself always to be alert and on guard that you never miss an opportunity to call for the blessing of another human being, especially another Child of Light. When you see one who is having a difficult time, remember to call to the Presence, and do not sit in judgment, but bless that one and pour forth your Light; then indeed you enter into the Pure Christ Light and rise into the octave of the Arisen Masters, and it is only thus attained. There is no short cut to Perfection, dear ones. The way may appear to be long but it is truly reached as you learn to manifest Perfection in your application of these simple Laws.

Never tire! Never tire! Never tire of making your application. When you feel that your attention is wandering, call it back and put it where it belongs! Dear ones, it is better to place your entire attention in making one call and being satisfied, than it is to worry and fret and be concerned about the activity of yourself and others.

Wisdom does not come to you at a single point, precious ones. You do not gain your ascension by calling to the Presence to raise you into your Mastery. You have not earned it, and you will not have what you have not earned. You cannot be cheated, because this is an actual

Law. *What you release comes back to you.* If you desire greater Illumination, call for it. If you desire greater Freedom, call for it and it will be given to you. *Nothing will be given to you without the asking and nothing will be given to you until you are ready to receive it*, and then at that moment the Heavens themselves will be opened and everything will be placed into your hands in an instant!

When the athlete runs the race he starts out to win with full confidence, with all his wind ready to go through victoriously, but as the race nears the end he strains and puffs and pulls in order to get through. So it is in this, dear ones, but contrary to your expression—"the first hundred is the hardest," it is quite the reverse and the last hundred decrees are the most difficult. Many times individuals have made such magnificent accomplishment and they become discouraged when so close to their full Victory, and then lay down on the job. Many times there have been such magnificent ones down through history who have made such magnificent accomplishment, yet failed to make their ascension only because they accepted that they had accomplished all they could accomplish, and lay down on the job. The number of blessed souls who pass out of embodiment coming within such a short distance of making their ascension is appalling! Hundreds of them who, with a little extra patience, a little extra determination, would so quickly make the last few steps into their Victory.

VI

OUR ELDER BROTHERS
by various Masters.

Unless individuals have the help of the Arisen Masters somewhere, sometime in their own lifestream, they cannot be strong enough to go on by themselves.

Remember always that your progress depends not only upon your own willingness to discipline yourself and your willingness to maintain rigid self-control at all times, but it also depends upon your call to the Great Host of Arisen Masters, the Legion of Light, and others who have perfected themselves, that their consciousness of Perfection may be the guiding way for you. You see, precious ones, it is not possible for anyone to make permanent achievement without the permanency of the Presence being released from the Presence. The permanent manifestation of the I AM Presence is the Arisen Master. Therefore, the Arisen Master and His radiation to you will give you the sustaining activity which you so much desire.

The Arisen Masters are real! They are the only reality in the physical octave of experience, the Full Reality, for in the physical octave you are still in the limited consciousness and you, of course, function where you find yourself, while the transcendent state of

Freedom the Masters live in is the only real, the only natural existence.

The greatest assistance that any student can receive from the Arisen Masters is the amplification of the radiation from his own I AM Presence, and blessed ones, never forget that it is the Presence that releases into your physical world all that you require, whether it be health, food, money, clothing, shelter, or whatever it may be. The I AM Presence is the storehouse and the great supplying Presence of the universe. As you call that Presence into action the assistance you receive from the Arisen Masters is the assistance of the Consciousness of Victory, the Consciousness of the Ascension, which even the Presence cannot release to you.

Remember, when an Arisen Master is called on, when His name is used in your decrees and affirmations, you give Him the opportunity of receiving even more happiness than He has already. Remember that the Arisen Masters work and live under the same Laws that govern you. Every time an Arisen Master is called upon, the call represents an opportunity for Him to pour forth more of Himself. Naturally, since you know the Law, the more a Master pours forth the more He receives. Not that We are looking forward to receiving anything, but it is Our Great Joy to be able to expand the Light in the hearts and minds of the children of our own planet, and be of assistance in raising the vibratory action of this your planet Earth.

Please feel free to continue calling upon Me and Those who work with Me. Remember, call your I AM Presence into action first, accepting God's Power working in and through your own being, then accept the helping hand of the Arisen Masters who, since They are Master, are able to amplify your call from the Arisen Master octave of Light. Amplify the Power further by calling the Great Cosmic Beings into action, and then be at Peace and know that it is done.

We do not dare sometimes to move into a condition

where humanity is too disturbed in their feelings, or all wrought up with their fears, doubts, and confusions, for if We move in We amplify them, which We cannot help due to laws of energy and vibration, and as those things are intensified the results are appalling. But you see the Cosmic Law is such that even though humanity today is still filled with doubts and fears, we have come forth and are moving in the physical octave, which certainly means that humanity in different parts of the Earth, as they feel Our radiation and Our presence, are being shocked into a sense of their own responsibility. As all things are being revealed to them they learn now and for all time that they are responsible for the condition of the world, for their own actions; that they and they alone create the chaos and confusion in which they move, and that they and they alone, through their calls to God, the I AM Presence, can raise themselves out of the mess.

The Cosmic Hour has arrived when humanity is going to have to know and recognize its Elder Brothers working with it, even though they do not see them with the outer sight. We are just as real—far more real then you are—because We do not have the illusion concerning life that you have. Thus We are able to render much more assistance and live a much more happy and full life than you are able to at your period of progress.

It is within the ability of each one individually to go as far as he wishes to go. I cannot tell you what you are to do. You have to determine that for yourself, and then you have to go on the journey by yourself. We can help you, but only to the extent that your are able to help yourself. When you make the call We can amplify it for you, but you must determine your own course of action and follow through with it. If you find you have made a mistake, give praise and thanks that you see you have made an error and then correct the mistake.

Do you realize what would occur were We to stand forth visible to everyone? Do you realize? O My dear children, it would be a catastrophe! Humanity couldn't

stand it. We have a difficult time as it is trying to
maintain peace and order in the world. If one of us were
to stand forth the confusion would be something! The
fear, the doubt! Just let your mind visualize what would
occur.

If you will turn your attention to your Presence and
make sincere application, you will see just how real We
are and just how real Wisdom guides Our actions and
Our words. Sometimes to the human mind these things
take a long time to develop, but that is an illusion, for
there is only now and here, and we are all together in this
Light just as much so today as we were years ago and as
we will be years from now.

If you want to be an Arisen Master you have to be
master of your own world. Seek how you may be the
most humble. Seek how you shall render the greatest
service. Place yourself as the servant of every other
human being, and if some one gets arrogant, turn to the
power of their God Presence, but do not let them walk
upon you!

Any individual who desires sincerely to make himself
a channel through which the Masters can pour their
words must of necessity love the Masters a great deal
and, therefore, as his love goes to Us We are constantly
in touch with such a one. You see, even though We are
arisen, We must obey Law; in fact, in regard to the
obedience to Law I could say much, but to continue:

The various ones who turn their attention to Us—and
remember, when the attention is turned in Love We
always respond—many times will see Us and feel us
coming to them and then We are able, in the release of
feeling, to cause them to receive certain messages,
although they are not able to receive the activity of
Dictations, which is the flashing of Letters of Living
Light before the All-Seeing Eye in the feeling world of
one who has been prepared especially to be such a channel. The message will always be phrased in the words of
the individual receiving the message but it will contain

Our radiation. The message may not always be completely accurate in detail, but as far as it does exist, the substance is usually accurate. One might question as to how it could not be called accurate if an Arisen Master released it. When We have a specific message to be given to a group of people, We do take care that the message is released accurately, but at such times as We have a specific message of encouragement of Love for one individual, the feeling which we release is the most important thing and, therefore, even if incorrectly received, still the perfection intended is accomplished. If you will think well upon this explanation which I have given you will understand perhaps many things which have confused you in the past. Remember, the Arisen Master is unlimited in any way, and remember always that the Master is able to select those with whom He wishes to work. It would be a sorry state of affairs indeed if there were not any channels We could use.

The question will come up, how is it possible for the Arisen Masters, apparently on the invisible or inner realms, to make apparently physical appearances with those still operating in physical bodies? How does the connection take place? Does the Arisen Master lower the vibratory action of His body until it becomes a physical body, or does the vibratory action of the individual's flesh body rise to the point where the individual is no longer in a physical body? The answer in both cases is no. The Arisen Master lowers the vibratory action of His body until it becomes visible to the increased vibratory action of the student. The student remains in his physical body and the Arisen Master remains in His Arisen Master body. They are both perfectly tangible to each other; however, should another individual in a physical body be standing near and be ignorant of the action taking place, if it were intended only for the benefit of the one receiving the Master's instruction, that one would in no way become aware of what was taking place. You will quickly see, therefore, the great reality of the Inner

Law, which is really the One Law, there is no other. All things are One. I AM All Things. Accept that consciousness. Dwell in it always.

The names of those who serve humanity are not important, and it is not necessary for the people of Earth to know them at this time. The names that you know them by at this time have merely been given for the purpose of convenience and are essential only for the matter of identification. Also, do not be confused by the similarity of appearances among the Masters.

Do not harbor the delusion that an Arisen Master is a physical being. An Arisen Master cannot be a physical being. An Arisen Master can be a tangible being, and is. Please understand this. You do not see the Arisen Master with your physical consciousness because your physical consciousness vibrates at a vibratory rate which is physical. If you wish to see an arisen Master you will raise your vibratory action to the place where it is no longer physical, and then you will see him. If a portion of your activity can be raised, such as your eyesight, your speech, your mind, your body (these can be raised together or separately), it will tune in automatically to the plane it seeks. There is nothing supernatural, nor am I some great being so far advanced beyond you that you can never attain. I am merely your Elder Brother who has gone before you and who has now returned to point the way, and what I have done you can do also. It is not easy, but it can and must be done.

*   *   *

It is true that there are quite a number of Arisen Masters in excess of the number of Arisen Lady Masters, but I wish you to understand unmistakably that the pathway to Perfection is no more difficult for one than for the other, because you see each one manifests many times as man and many times as woman. The determination of the individual is the deciding factor.

It is true that many times while the individual is functioning in a masculine body he will perhaps make greater progress than he would in a feminine body, because in the feminine form the individual functions through the realm of feeling to such a large extent, but dear ones, that is no excuse for losing control of your feelings, and I wish to caution you about this very carefully, for there have been oh so many times the blessed ladies have said: "Well, you see it is so much more difficult for us and that kind of excuses us for making these mistakes." That is not so, for it is no more difficult for one than for another!

*   *   *

Dear ones, when you read of our accomplishments or when you hear the stories of the blessed souls who have led the humanity of this Earth from one accomplishment to another, oftentimes it seems to you that the activity of accomplishment comes about very swiftly, that there are no dull spots in between, so to speak, that everything is very rapid, in perfect order, and goes forward to attainment so swiftly. I should like to correct that impression, which is so often given by writers of books and tellers of stories, because naturally they are concerned only with the important events, but, dear ones, you must know that in every great accomplishment there is a preceding period of days and days, sometimes weeks, months, even years, which brings that event to pass. Thus you must see that above all things you must have patience.

You—An Arisen Master In Embryo

The Law of this Planet now makes possible the coming forth of the Arisen Masters in their tangible bodies. It is now becoming possible because blessed individuals are now being accepted by the great Arisen

Host as Masters in embryo. Each of you, as a conscious student of the Light, as a conscious member of the Divine Family, each of you is an Arisen Master in embryo, and as you recognize these Great Laws and put them into action, you move forward until you stand face to face with the Arisen Masters, and you go on and on rendering greater and greater service to your brothers and sisters until a time where your service to humanity will have raised you into the Perfection where discord and inharmony cease to exist.

Nothing Of The Psychic

There is nothing psychic or spiritualistic that takes place from the Arisen Masters' standpoint. Remember always, the Arisen Masters come from an octave where everything is wholly Pure and Perfect, and coming from that octave of Perfection there is nothing psychic, hypnotic or spiritualistic about anything they do. However, in coming into the atmosphere of Earth it is necessary for every Arisen Master to come through the psychic realm. Now a great percentage of that has been removed, due to the sincere calls of the students in the past few years, but there is still a very great part of the psychic realm left which can act in the world of the individual. This the Arisen Master must penetrate, coming through in His own Wall of Protection in order to reach the student with His radiation or His own tangible presence.

Many times individuals are misled, oh so seriously, by the psychic forces because mankind unillumined longs very much to receive the tangible presence of the Masters, if only to satisfy their own curiosity and disbelief; and longing for that turns their attention many times to the psychic realm, which has nothing whatever to do with the Arisen Masters or the Pure Light of the Christ. Your repudiation of the powers of the psychic realm can only come about when you turn sincerely to the I AM Presence for then you are enfolded in your own automatic protection, which is established when you call directly to your own I AM self.

When the Arisen Master comes to the individual He comes through a Ray of Light similar to and corresponding with that same ray of Light from the Presence which enfolds the individual who is sincere in calling to the Presence. Thus you will see that there is nothing at all of the psychic or the spiritualistic activity going on, for that is always a very uncertain activity and whatever is accomplished is of a very uncertain nature. By that I mean to say that promptings which come through the psychic realm are always blurred, dark, and confused, and so-called mediums and individuals who have turned their attention into that very unhappy state of consciousness find themselves always trying to tell people's fortunes or prognosticate or, of course, prevaricate.

Use, use, use, the motto of the Great White Brotherhood: "TO KNOW, TO DARE, TO DO, AND TO BE SILENT." Listen to that motto. Let it speak in your hearts. Mold your actions accordingly, and know that no harm can befall you, and you will see that the Light, when understood, without fanaticism and without pressure, always protects its own. Be the fulfillment of that motto and you will be the fulfillment of the Law.

VII

OBEDIENCE TO GOD PRINCIPLE
by Serapis Bey.

Every student on the pathway should begin at once to realize that Life is Eternal. There is no death. Knowing then that Life flows on forever and that it is only by your conscious mastery of that Life that one may enter the Arisen state, should determine each one to make his or her maximum application each waking moment. Unless each moment is spent in conscious adoration and praise to the I AM Presence, the Source of all Life, or otherwise spent in releasing energy to bless mankind, then that moment is wasted and gone forever. True, there is no time or space. What a blessing to know that. Knowing that, we realize that no matter what mistakes may have been made in the past, one can instantly stop, turn and face his own radiant I AM, the Presence of the Living God within him. In doing that consciously, constantly, do you accept the Oneness of all things; so also do you accept that time is only now and that space is only here, for such indeed is the case.

In My activity of Love and Blessing to mankind upon this planet I have endeavored to assist in many ways. There are many who feel that My discipline is extremely severe, but actually I have never disciplined any. My

74

instruction to the individual has always caused him to wish to discipline himself. Self-discipline is the only type of discipline that can exist in the New Golden Age. Obedience to form will not be required. Obedience to God Principle is required eternally. "I AM that obedience to the God Principle within me. I AM the Presence of Good knowing all things, thinking all things, being all things which are constructive."

Those who have a desire to bring forth music, art, or literature of one form or another will find that I am very anxious to assist and will do so if they will turn their attention to Me. Each individual must feel free to do that according to the prompting he receives from his own I AM Presence.

There is no individual who can be the authority for any other individual. This does not mean that authority cannot exist in the outer world. It does exist. Authority is always God-given. To speak with the voice of Authority is to realize that "I AM God's Power speaking through my voice." To misuse authority is to misuse God's Power. Those in authority should always consider the good of the greatest number. If, instead, they consider their own private good, they are misusing their authority and it will be taken from them. He who would win authority must find how best he can serve the multitude. The service to the multitude is made, not by making the way for the many, but rather by expanding the Light within the many. That is the only true service to mankind. The one who can do that more than another will have the greater authority.

There is no competition. Such a word is merely human creation. There can be no competition in a world made by One Creator. That Creator is God, I AM. One part of God does not vie against another part. Things opposite to each other many times are merely one action.

In understanding the Trinity, or the Father, Son, and Holy Ghost, you must understand that the same principle is in action. Action and reaction together create the third principle of action, which is the combining of both, all three being One. If individuals will see this they will stop trying to interfere with other individuals. I tell you again, competition does not exist! There is only One—that One is Light. Anyone consciously seeking that Light will find it, for the pathway is open. I AM is the Fullness of that Light.

I AM, or God Principle, is not owned or controlled by any group of people. I AM is God. The teaching of I AM can never be withheld from individuals. Each one would do well to contemplate that very earnestly. Each one will also do well to realize that only by living within his own world will perfection ever come forth for the balance of mankind. You cannot interfere with other people's business, and your business is never their business. Individuals are raised up over their fellows so that they may have an opportunity of giving more. If that opportunity is misused, the most tremendous failure is the result. Let the one who seeks authority for himself think first upon the responsibility which he has at the moment. Authority and responsibility go hand in hand. Do not attempt to take on yourself the responsibility of another individual. You are free God beings. Maintain yourself in Harmony, in Peace, with a blessing to all mankind, and you will remain free beings.

Freedom is man's natural estate. Anything less than freedom is man's own creation. This country guarantees freedom. It will not be kept unless people will learn to respect that freedom and to desire that freedom to such an extent that they will defend it. If America will keep herself clear of foreign entanglements she will remain the Cup of Light for all the world in the future; then those in America will be privileged to carry that Light to the rest of the world.

You must learn to maintain rigid control of your feelings. To feel violently about anything is usually to act quickly without wisdom. Before releasing any feeling you must learn to be calm. Then whatever feeling you release will be qualified with Divine Love if you call it forth that way. Many times students, because of their alertness in receiving a prompting, react violently. The Arisen Masters are not violent, neither is the one upon the road to Mastery. Violence is human. If you receive a prompting from your Presence or from an Arisen Master, be calm and self-contained, even though the prompting be very powerful. To become excited is to move away from the oneness you have established with your God Presence. Be master always. Learn to direct your energy consciously. Do not waste it.

You will never reach the Arisen state unless you claim it for yourself, nor will you ever reach it unless you accept it for all others. The Arisen state is a state of sustained Perfection. The outer world can have perfection but it is not sustained. To call forth sustained Perfection for the outer world is to raise that Perfection into the Arisen state. The Arisen state, which all must reach, must be reached consciously. It is a matter of energy released.

The individual who maintains life in his body indefinitely will find it much easier to be of service to the Arisen Host. Your desire should not be to leave your body but to spend every moment in your body well. You are the authority for what takes place in your world. You are also responsible for what takes place there. Do not be afraid of responsibility. Claim your God authority. You as a part of God have infinite right to command Perfection to come forth everywhere. You also have infinite right to command that imperfection cease to exist. But you have no right to command in God's name that freedom be removed from another individual; this cannot be. Everyone must have freedom to make his own progress according to the Light within him.

Much has been set aside for the student on the pathway, but never will the student's freedom be set aside. To do that in one instance would be to destroy the entire scheme of things and the universe would cease to exist. The solution to every problem is found in releasing a feeling of Divine Love to everyone. Divine Love is a substance—it is the Substance of Light. It is Intelligent, for it knows what to do, and when you send forth a feeling of Divine Love you cooperate in the highest way possible with your own God Presence.

Divine Love knows no barrier. Remember, a feeling of Divine Love and Compassion sent to an individual is never a feeling of criticism, antagonism or judgment. Nor is it in any way a feeling of superiority over the individual. Rather is it a feeling of Gratitude, a feeling of Compassion, a feeling of Oneness, which is a blessing to the one receiving the Divine Love sent forth, and an even greater blessing to the one who sends it forth. To so train yourself that you can release no feeling but Divine Love would be to train yourself to live in a Beautiful Garden of Light eternally. When you have trained yourself to live the Law of Love so that no feeling but one of Love can ever leave you, then will you be worthy of the ascension.

There is no short cut to the ascension. Every individual will make the ascension by his own application. He will do it either in this embodiment or another. The energy released between embodiments can also be used. The ascension, however, must be made from the physical side of life. You make your own ascension when you are prepared to do so. The limited understanding of the human does not know when that preparation is complete. The I AM Presence does know and will inform you.

Do not lean upon individuals. If you are truly grateful for the lesson which a teacher has given you, you will prove it best by applying that lesson. To fawn upon one and to court favor is but to display your own lack of control over your feelings.

So many in the outer world feel that Jesus, in His magnificent ministration, could not be equalled. Jesus Himself constantly said otherwise. There are many who say that Saint Germain cannot be equalled. Saint

Germain has not told you that, nor will He. There are many who say that Godfre Ray King cannot be equalled. He has not told you that, nor will He. Your loyalty and love to your teacher is best expressed by your comprehension and expansion of the teaching.

The feeling that is predominant within any individual at any given time is the feeling that he gives to others, for it is an action in his own feeling world which sets into action a like activity in the feeling world of everyone with whom he comes in contact. Also, in a lesser degree, it sets up that same activity in the feeling world of any to whom his attention is directed. You will quickly see your great responsibility to feel Love, Joy, and Peace constantly, particularly in this trying period of the world's unfoldment.

Peace is an activity which seems to have been forgotten by humanity. This is largely because man feels that peace is a lack of activity, whereas war is activity; peace then would be a negative state. Peace, when understood and properly called forth, will expand into the most magnificent activity of the New Golden Age. This can come forth!

To accuse an individual who wants Peace of being a communist is one of the most foolish things that can be done. You should know, as students, that every individual, regardless of what doctrine he appears to follow, is one of God's children. It is your obligation, as students on the pathway, to be strong enough to contact any individual and raise him into a position on the Pathway. You do not have to defend the Light, the Light will defend you. Make yourself ever more worthy of greater Light, then will you receive ever greater Perfection.

The Cosmic Cycle has now swung past the point where those who represent the Light can be publicly put to death. There are perhaps some who would like to do so, but they are very few. Mankind upon this planet all long for the Light. You, as one individual, can assist in

giving that Light to them. You are your own authority in
so doing. Mankind needs Light. They do not need forms
to follow. They need to understand that *the Presence of
the Living God, I AM, is within them.* Without that
Understanding they are lost in the darkness of human
creation; with that Understanding they can go forth into
Victory.

How can one individual expect others to be interested
in what he is doing if he is not interested in it himself?
Those things which you have determined upon to do
should be worthy of your full attention. If they are not,
find something else to do. The Law of Life demands your
full attention. Sometimes students ask how it is possible
for them to give their full attention to the expansion of
this Light and at the same time maintain an activity in
the business world. A little contemplation on the Oneness
of all things and the activity of Light will clear up this
matter for the sincere seeker.

Those things which you have determined upon to do,
do them perfectly. Inasmuch as you understand yourself
to be a part of God, you must see that God will not be
employed upon a trivial matter. Accept your
responsibility as a God Being. You will never advance
very far unless you accept your responsibility. Additional
responsibility accepted in wisdom always brings an expansion of Light in the world of the individual accepting
the responsibility.

Do not fear cataclysms, wars, accidents or destructive
activities of the human. Even though you receive a
prompting that a destructive thing is about to take place
does not mean that it has to take place. If you receive
such a prompting it is your signal to go to work to stop
the destruction! The same is true with individuals. If you
see one about to perform an error you have the authority
to command that the error be not performed. Your
command should be to your own God Presence. Then,
accepting the power of this Presence in action, turn your
attention away from the individual and know that the

Perfection will come forth. The manifestation of that Perfection may not appear instantly, but your call will ultimately bring forth the perfection you desire for the other.

Do not be concerned with appearances. When you find it possible to be of assistance to another you should be extremely humble. Assistance given in all humbleness is always a God activity. Be of good cheer. The Glory and Perfection you so much desire for others is as near to you as the Power of Love from your own heart.

*   *   *

Thou All-enfolding Presence of Infinity, O Great Blazing Light, I AM, we Love Thee and stand at-one with Thee, accepting Thy Full God Power within us now and forever. Keep us eternally aware of our obligation to other Brothers and Sisters on the Pathway that we may give in loving service to them always. Here before this Altar do I stand. Beside me are the Wings of Life which, unfurled, take one into the Glory and the Fullness of the Everlasting God. Behind me is the Open Doorway into the Fullness of Life. I AM the Life, the Truth, and the Way.

VIII

THE FIRE OF FORGIVENESS
by Urlando.

From My far home I come to you for the first time in many thousands of years. I have been known to you many times. I have many names. I have many forms. In a far day of long ago I worked with each of you in establishing a portion of the great civilization of Lemuria. At that time the land where your present City of San Francisco is located was a portion of the vast continent of Mu, and the great civilization that stood in this self-same spot represented the Golden Gateway to the East instead of the Golden Gateway to the West. At that time, what is now much of the coastline of California was the eastern coast of Lemuria. Water stretched everywhere from the bay area down through Death Valley, clear into a portion of Arizona and New Mexico and downward finally connecting with what is now the Gulf of California. Many of the mountains existing today were not in existence at that time, and there upon that ancient shore a mighty civilization rose to great heights and fell, due to the turning away from the Great Presence of Almighty God.

I have come to you tonight through a great tunnel of Light which connects My star to the Earth, as you have

observed. I am a Messenger of the Gods and you have
seen Me many times with winged sandals. I have been
known as Mercury.

My activity has always been one of very close contact
with the humanity of Earth. That close contact was
established and maintained until approximately 4,000
years ago, at which time I withdrew. There were many in
the Greek civilization who knew Me well. Also, I was
known during the Egyptian, the Atlantean, and the Lemurian
civilizations. The Cosmic Law compelled Me to
go forth and leave the Children of Earth to their own
discord, and not until your lifestreams coming together in
this fashion with mine, was it possible for Me to be drawn
forth.

If you wish My assistance call to Me. I would prefer
that you use the name "Urlando" in so doing. In fact, I
would prefer that you do not use other names for they
have been filled with human consciousness and bring to
individuals many pictures that are untrue. You will find
My speed in answer to your calls can be something that
can be very valuable, if your desire is good.

I wish to talk a little bit about the atomic structure in
the thought world, as well as in the world of feeling, so
that you may better understand just how the activity of
the Fire of Forgiveness goes into action, and also how
you may more clearly realize and appreciate the
tremendous necessity for holding absolute control over
the feelings and thoughts.

Thought is composed of atoms and is propelled into
its form by love, which is, of course, the molding and
directing consciousness throughout the universe just as
much as any physical object in the outer world.
Remember, that a thought-form called into action is a
tangible thing, and though there are not sufficient atoms
in it usually to be seen by the outer eyesight, nonetheless
the thought held in the mind draws the atoms to that
pattern and the thought becomes a thing.

Even a vicious thought or a thought of complete

destruction is a thing, and is created and held together through the activity of Love. Now it may seem to you very odd that a vicious thought could be the result of love, but remember, I did not say that it was the result of love, but love is the force that created it. Now a vicious thought is usually brought forth by self love—by the individual having his attention upon himself and trying to justify himself more than he wishes to pour forth love to life everywhere he finds it, and of course, love to his own Presence of Life. So you see, even misdirected energy comes about in some measure through the activity of love, and any form that is created must have love in order to be sustained or created even for an instant.

After a form has been created in the thought world it remains to act in the thought world as a living, breathing entity, sometimes very small, sometimes quite large, depending upon the power given to it, and it remains to act that way in the thought world until such time as the original decree which created the thought, or the original impulse which caused the thought, is completely withdrawn and the Fire of Forgiveness is called upon. Thus you will see that a thought held in the mind of a small child and then dismissed may not even be thought again for years and years, yet all at once it may again come to the surface as the individual again goes through a similar experience or is impelled through some inner prompting to turn his attention in the same direction. The thought reoccurs even after years, and thus you see that thought becomes a very permanent thing.

There is only one way in which the thoughts of the average individual can be raised and purified out of the old habit or momentum gathered through childhood and adolescence and early maturity, and that is by using the Fire of Forgiveness through the mental world. Now the activity of the Fire of Forgiveness through the mental world releases Light through the electrons which compose the atoms, and which serve as a nucleus of love which hold the atoms together. Thus, as the electronic force of the atom is increased the negative force which composes the atom no longer has as much power, a certain amount of off balance occurs in each atom and the atoms fly back into their original purity, where they are repolarized and are freed from any human consciousness. The release of the Fire of Forgiveness is the activity which performs that service and it is one of the most magnificent helps which humanity can know anything about.

In order to intensify the Light within the atom or to charge the electron with more of its own energy, the Fire of Forgiveness must have some energy to work with in order to do this. This energy flows directly from the Presence and is released through the activity of the individual by his call when the heart and the head of the individual combine in pattern and force to bring about the necessary result.

When the call is made for the use of the Fire of Forgiveness from an intellectual standpoint a very small portion of the work is done, and on the other hand, when the call is made only from the feeling, the directing intelligence is not able to guide the work of the Fire of Forgiveness to the point where a habit may be completely erased. That is to say, although the Fire of Forgiveness would act in full power, the mental pattern would be very easily reformed as the record would remain. Thus you will see that it is imperative when you call to the Presence for the use of the Fire of Forgiveness that you call with a sincere, determined consciousness, knowing the activity which will take place.

Speaking further with reference to the creations of the human mind and consciousness I would say: When you as an individual feel discord in your world, it is a clear indication that the atoms which compose your world are beginning to lose their polarity, but they are losing it not as a result of an increase of Light within the atom but rather as a result of the decrease of the Light within the atom, which slows down the vibratory action within each atom. Thus the feeling or physical world will express pain and discomfort and the mental world will become confused. This happens when the individual permits discord to come into his world; and that discord, unless straightened out by greater Light, will increase and spread itself just like a growth of infectious disease, for it will race from atom to atom, slowing down the vibratory rate until what was perhaps once only in the mental world, goes into the feeling world and the physical world, and the individual will have sickness, caused wholly by discord driven in which the individual failed to remove while still in the invisible state.

The need of holding harmony in the feeling cannot be over-emphasized. You must bear in mind that you are using energy constantly. Every time you think a thought, every time you breathe a breath, you are using God's pure and perfect energy. You are the qualifier at all times as to how that energy shall affect you and others, for it comes to you pure and perfect, but you are the qualifier. Therefore, if you determine now to take the reins of authority, stand guard over your mental and feeling world, stand guard over your speech, and discipline yourself, you will find very quickly that you will be a happier, freer, keener, and more useful being. You will have taken a great step on the road to Mastery.

It is imperative that you recognize a destructive or negative thing when it first drives in. You see, just a little doubt, a fear, a little greed, a little unkindness, will so quickly expand itself. Those are the things to watch. Watch them while they are yet small and nip them quickly before they can expand and increase.

Now in exactly the same manner the good things also expand, so when you have a feeling of Love, of Peace, of Joy, turn your attention to it and let it expand. Those things are the natural activity of life and, therefore, you will have less difficulty in increasing those if you turn your attention to them and take it off the disturbing conditions. But remember, when you feel a disturbing condition, whether it be mental, emotional, or physical, sincerely and determinedly call to your Presence for the use of the Fire of Forgiveness and ask that whatever has occurred may be forgiven, that the Fire of Forgiveness be used to intensify the Light within the electron of each atom that is causing the disturbance.

No matter what the conditions may be, you as students of life may quickly overcome them. It has been said that if a great many people were gathered together in one building, none of them students of the Light, and one should come who was a student, that one could raise the activity of the others, and that is positively true. So many times one will take the consciousness—well, from this moment on I shall be kind, happy, joyous—and then something will come up and that one will make the call and it doesn't work, but I tell you *your I AM Presence always works*! If you make the call and you do not have the results you should have, go on and be more determined than ever, releasing nothing but Love, Happiness, Beauty, and Harmony!

SAINT GERMAIN:

Without the knowledge of the Law of Life men are very blind. They do not see because their consciousness has not been opened to the world of cause and effect. Humanity still feels that it is possible to perform some act or to release some energy and not suffer the consequences and, of course, that is ridiculous, for the Law of Cause and Effect is absolute.

There is only one activity that can raise you above the Law of Cause and Effect and that is the Fire of Forgiveness—the Law of Forgiveness—which will raise you above the necessity of experiencing the result of your previous mistakes. The Law of Forgiveness, of course, is active only when the individual is sincere. Just calling forth the Fire of Forgiveness will never in the world release the individual from experiencing his own discord until in his own heart he has called for forgiveness and wishes sincerely to be forgiven. Let Me assure you, dear ones, that if you do not forgive others you yourself will never be forgiven. The Law·of Life will see to it that whatever you send forth will come back to you, and thus you will see that when you as an individual send forth a sincere desire to be forgiven, that in itself is the activity of forgiveness which dissolves the discord.

You as individuals never have to use a destructive force. Remember that! You cannot do that and remain a being of Light and Love. Never think for a minute that you can escape the Great Law of Cause and Effect in that respect, for if your human tells you that you are justified in destroying another, that feeling or thought will ultimately cause your own destruction. There is no escaping it! The evil in the world is in the process of turning upon itself and destroying itself. Thus, men who are evil and who desire evil will be at war with others who are evil and desire evil until they have destroyed themselves; but up out of that will come the Children of Light who are Good and desire Good. They cannot be destroyed. The Truth is Triumphant now and forever! THE LIGHT OF GOD NEVER FAILS!

You as an Individualized Flame of Life have the quality of individual expression, that is to say, you have the power of qualifying individually according to your own experience, according to your own comprehension, those things which you observe. Thus you will see, the individual whose experience is quite vast will qualify one thing quite differently than an individual whose experience is somewhat limited. The act itself, of course, would remain the same, but the power of qualification is very tremendous, and I assure you, dear ones, that when an individual misqualifies something it is no less real to that one misqualifying than to another who qualifies it perfectly.

You have all perhaps observed individuals who

become ill periodically—they just have such a terrible time it would seem. Now the truth of the matter is, they are not ill at all, but they have, through appearances and habit, qualified a certain amount of energy as having the power to make them ill, or some certain act, or some certain food that would bring about a short periodical illness. Now the onlooker would be inclined to say they are just pretending, and yet they are not pretending for that energy qualified will act, and is perfectly real to the individual, although those outside the individual's world would not be able to observe it at all. That is true particularly with children. Remember, their power of qualification is just as great as yours and if they are permitted to build imprints of feeling ill or some other negative condition it will act in their worlds.

It is imperative that you call to the Presence to control your power of qualification. Say many times: "Beloved I AM Presence, seize my power of qualification. Let me qualify all things with Light." That will very swiftly raise you into a position where no matter what happens, you will find yourself free from limitations. There is nothing more important, aside from calling to your Presence, than the keeping of the power of your qualification charged with Light and filled with Love.

Remember, when the I AM Presence releases Its energy to flow on its way in your world, that energy is not qualified at all. It flows on just as perfect as Life itself, in fact, it *is* Life, Light—it is your own Life—and when it touches your world it takes on the quality of your world, just as there are many stones which, when they contact the body of an individual (I am speaking of precious stones and semi-precious stones), take on the quality of the individual wearing them. Thus, some stones will take on luster and others will grow very dull when worn by someone qualifying negatively.

The power of qualification is a very great one and your privilege in calling the Presence to control that for you is very great indeed. I would particularly urge the student at this point to use the Law of Forgiveness—the Fire of Forgiveness—and ask for harmony to be released into your feeling world, and then watch closely your power of qualification.

Another important point: Examine your worlds and clear out quickly, by using the Fire of Forgiveness, those wrong mental conclusions which are arrived at through partial information only!

Know always that no matter what may have occurred in the past—no matter what errors you may have made, even today—it is never too late to turn to your Presence, when the heart is sincere. Always you can say: "O Beloved I AM Presence, forgive me," and go into the Father's House to receive His Blessing, His Love, His Bounteous Protection. When you are sincere in your heart you can go into the arms of your Presence—you cannot go when you are not sincere—but when you sincerely say: "Father, Thou Great and Blessed I AM Presence, forgive me. I call on the Law of Forgiveness which I AM. Blaze up though me the Fire of Forgiveness and take me again into Thy Heart." Then, dear ones, you go forth forever into that realm of Peace and Purity which is your eternal birthright, the Victory of Life Supreme.

Think of it, dear ones! You are not damned eternally by your mistakes. The Law of Cause and Effect, however righteous, however just, is completely set aside for you when you turn to that Great Presence of Light which beats your heart, and call on the Law of Forgiveness, the purifying Flame of Love.

As you use the Law of Forgiveness, the Fire of Forgiveness, you release Freedom to act upon this planet.

The Fire of Forgiveness

I AM the Fire of Forgiveness, the Violet Flame Divine
From the Heart of God the Father I come,
Through Me, O children your Vict'ry is won!
Call to Me, Love Me, that I may blaze through,
Consuming mistakes, bringing Life, ever new.
I do not condemn, neither judge, nor condone,
Come into My Heart, O children, My own!
Abide here, My dear ones all pure, all free,
I hold you fore'er in the heart of Me!
The Presence of Saint Germain am I,
Releasing this Flame to purify.
O let Me expand through your heart, my son,
To enfold the earth, that her Peace may come.
I AM the Power of Light from the Sun,
Consuming mistakes, raising all to the One.
I heal, I bless, I AM Pure Love
From the Heart of God, the Father above.
O children of earth, from the Father's Heart too
Let My Power of Light ever blaze through you!

I AM the Law of Forgiveness, the Violet Flame Divine.

—B.C.—

IX

LIFE, LIGHT, GOD—ALL ONE

by Hilarion.

I am supremely happy in coming to you this evening for I have had many individuals through whom I have worked in the past in My service, which has always been to assist the mankind of this Earth, and yet not until now was the way opened for Me to come to you. I rejoice at the great progress that has been made and I am extremely happy that the way is still open for the Victory to come forth in America.

In adding My radiation to that which has already been given to you it is My wish that you observe very clearly some of the action which will take place in the coming days. Those of mankind who are aware of the Arisen Masters have long been quite familiar with My activity and many have known that I have existed to various ones in the scientific fields and in the field of research. But I have also existed in many other ways and My coming to you tonight is to inform you of certain things which perhaps you do not know.

Remember always that Light is the One. Light is substance, it is intelligence, it is action in which Light, Life, and God are the same. These three are one. Knowing that, and knowing also that "I AM" is one with all things, the individual will quickly see that precipitation is no myth. By focusing the attention and the feeling as steady streams of energy upon any given desire, that desire will manifest as a tangible physical thing. It is impossible for it not to manifest when the desire is sincere, the attention steady, and the feeling determined. Precipitation, however, to those in the physcial realm, will seem for a number of years yet to be a very strange activity, and yet it will become known and there are many people who, when they learn of the I AM Presence, will be enabled to precipitate almost instantly anything that they desire.

Those who have in previous embodiments worked consciously with the nature elementals, particularly working with the God of Gold or the God of Nature, will find precipitation in this embodiment a very natural activity for them. Others will find that they have to work with a great deal more effort in order to arrive at the place where some will naturally come; but what a joy to know that in the I AM Presence there is no time or space, and thus, no matter how many times an individual calls forth the activity of precipitation, if he will accept that there is such an activity, and recognizing neither time nor space, enter into the oneness of which he is a part, he will quickly see that precipitation can become an everyday occurrence.

The great obstacle to the precipitation of any object is man's almost continual longing to observe a manifestation. Unless that longing is removed, precipitation cannot become a normal part of the individual's activity, and right now, conditions being as they are in the outer world, We will give no assistance in that direction to one who has not learned to control the longing for manifestation.

I am sure you will be pleased to know that before many years have passed the invention of destructive implements of warfare and destructive chemical combinations will become unknown upon this planet. Means are being used at the present time to remove the memory of certain destructive combinations and activities from the minds of various ones in the world that might, in a few years time unless this were done, release very great destruction upon this planet. You will have cause in the months ahead to rejoice greatly that this has been done. Your calls in that direction can be of great assistance for there is much energy that We still need.

There is a new means of transportation which is being prepared right now in America which is so revolutionary that the two channels bringing it forth are afraid to release it. I am working to see that they will be protected until what they have to release can come forth without interference. I believe it is safe to tell you that this new means of transportation to which I have referred is a vehicle that does not use wheels anywhere in its construction, and is similar to those used in the Atlantean civilization. The speed of these new vehicles will be so tremendous as to cause mankind to reorder their thinking along those lines completely, and yet they will be the safest vehicles yet released.

So many times it has amused me to observe that humanity for the most part think of the scientist as a cold, calculating, nonemotional individual. Really, a scientist is neither cold nor calculating, if he is a good scientist, and although he may have to govern his emotions in some respects, in many respects the average scientist could improve greatly. Many of them unknowingly will prevent magnificent things coming through by the very fact that they have not learned to govern their emotions.

There is one thing which I must ask of those of you who wish to receive assistance from My Ray and that is that you learn to speak with great accuracy; that you learn to think with accuracy, and feel with accuracy. So many times I have noticed the inclination of many who are calling to Us in the Arisen state to exaggerate, and that is never the course of Mastery, for to be Master one must be perfectly balanced at all times and absolutely accurate. Realize always, it is not necessary always to disclose your activities to your friends, but it is necessary even in the withholding of information to be absolutely truthful and absolutely accurate. So many times I have heard really blessed ones say something to this effect: "O I like this a thousand times more than something else," or, "This is so much greater than something else," etc. That is not the wise method of procedure. It is better to be accurate with feeling than just to have feeling. You will find when you have trained yourself to accuracy that you will not have to go back and correct people's impressions as to what you have said. Remember always, that the feeling behind a word is more important than the word; however, unless you choose your words with care, if an individual does not know you well he perhaps will be unable to tune into your feeling as readily as he contacts your spoken word; therefore, a very wrong impression can be given by one individual to another when the one speaking is generous with his feeling but perhaps a little careless in his choice of words.

This does not mean that you should become overconscious in your speech, for speech in itself is but the human method of expressing ideas. At the same time, however, it is wise, as My Beloved Brother, the Venetian, has told you, to speak clearly and distinctly and always to speak with great Love. Let Me tell you something. There is no information, there is no mechanical contrivance, there is no great scientific advancement that has ever come forth without great Love, and every true scientist loves his work very dearly, and the ray of Light pouring from his heart, combined with the powerful ray of concentration from his head, is a portion of the precipitation activity which permits a thing to come forth. The scientist who does not love his work is not willing to discipline himself to pour forth love to that which he is undertaking, and will never bring forth anything of great account.

It is Saint Germain's wish that I tell you a little

tonight about the activity of the creation of your planet
and various changes through which it has passed and
through which it must pass before it rises into its
permanent state of perfection. The universe is in reality
but a great atom, and every atom is in reality but a tiny
universe, for all things that exist, exist through Love, and
Love is the Power that creates the atom and maintains it,
and it is also the power that creates the universe and
maintains it, for the universe is but many atoms all
operating in perfect order.

This great universe of which your planet is such an
infinitesimal part is a universe of great Light that is
constantly expanding. Greater and greater Light always
pours forth from the Great Central Sun, separating out
into space, forming new worlds in your system of worlds
and ever taking back into itself that which has fulfilled its
allotted span of existence; and by the activity of the
inflowing outflowing essence of Love, must again
become one with itself so that creation may go on
indefinitely.

Really, to look within your heart is to understand
the vastness of all space, and to contemplate the words "I
AM" is to make yourself Master of Substance, Energy,
and Vibration. Thus, as Master, you can move anywhere
you choose throughout the universe, knowing all things.
If you will dwell upon the idea that the Universe and God
are one and the same, you will begin to comprehend "I
AM that I AM." Then when you make the statement "I
AM the Open Door which no man can shut," you will see
whereby you have released the Power which enables you
to walk through the veil, standing within the Great
Central Sun and controlling as Master all manifested
things. Law and Order being the first rule, you will
quickly see that when one has entered into the I AM
Consciousness one becomes incapable of being in the
wrong place at any time.

When the planet was first formed it came forth as the
result of a direct series of Rays and Charges of Light from

the Great Central Sun. Your planet is in reality a Great Being and also is part of a Great Being, and yet again another part of still a greater Being. Remember that Light everywhere is Substance, Intelligence, and Action.

The development of mankind upon any given planet or world always passes through certain phases in which the individualized consciousness of each one is given a chance to expand the fullness of itself and thus pay back to Life, the only Source, the eternal debt one owes to Life. The payment of that debt is always made in service to another. Thus you will see in the true understanding of the words "I AM" you not only take the responsibility for yourself but you accept the responsibility of assisting all mankind to take their own responsibility. When sufficient of humanity upon any given planet have learned the Law of the One, the Law of Love, and obey it, the planet itself rises in vibratory action, it emits greater and greater Light and many times actually changes its relative position in regard to other planets, moving ever on a higher and higher spiral.

This may seem startling to some of you when I tell you that your planet Earth is now moving in nine directions at once. You may not see how this is possible but I assure you it is. Very soon now will come the great change and that will be a time of great rejoicing for all who understand and who will use their I AM Presence. From that moment on the planet Earth will emit greater Light and will actually rise physically into an orbit that is quite a little different from the one it now occupies. The seven Great Kumaras, Who have assisted the mankind of earth and without Whose assistance the people of earth would still be in great darkness, have all originally come from Venus. They are to Venus the same as the Chohans of the Rays are to your planet, and the same as the seven Great Elohim of Creation are to the Universe.

If you will recall that there are two secret Rays operating upon your planet at the present time you will see that the activity is necessary during the coming changes, and when the changes have been completed those Rays, which are a steadying influence during that time, will be withdrawn. One of those Rays has been established in the Bering Strait, the other upon what is known as the Island of Fire. Those Rays and the action of them will increase the actual vibratory action of this planet and some of that action all of you have felt or will feel. It is nothing to become alarmed about.

The permanent Golden Age is very near at hand. We in the Arisen state are longing for the day when We can come forth freely upon the surface of the Earth to give our instruction to the humanity who have learned obedience to their own God Presence. How foolish it is for man to go on seeking to destroy when, by the practice of Love, of Kindness, and Humility, destruction would never be necessary and mankind united at last would build without ceasing the greatest civilization of all time. So many will not listen, however, until they are driven and driven down and down to the very brink of complete despair. Only then will they stop and listen to reason which is the greatest reason of all time, and the only reason, the only Law that ever can or ever will exist. That reason is "I AM."

The further one advances in study or in progress of any sort, the more simplified the understanding becomes. Thus I can say to you that when you truly understand the full meaning of the words "I AM" all other knowledge will be nonessential, for "I AM" contains all things.

Do you know something? I am really a very joyous individual, although very often I do not show My true feeling, still My radiation is always one of Great Joy and great accomplishment. Is it not magnificent to know that one can enter into the I AM Presence and there always find perfect Peace, magnificent God Ideas, Divine Love, and Joy in action? No matter what the appearance world may say, still can each individual enter into the Father's House and there, shutting the door against all disturbance, remain calm and at ease, master of all things.

*   *   *

Most Radiant and Holy One, Thou Infinite I AM
Presence, before Thy Blazing Fire we stand,
acknowledging ourselves within Thee, ever seeking to
expand more of Thy Perfection, ever calling to release
more of Thy Light to the Children of Earth. I AM One
with Thee. Do Thou expand Thy Perfection through me
at all times. May the Peace that comes with Perfect
Action now enter into the hearts and minds of all
mankind to fill them with Light, with the ecstasy of
Divine Love, and the Full Understanding of the Oneness
of all things.

X

ENERGY AND VIBRATION
by the Maha Chohan.

It will be My privilege to talk to you for a short while concerning the laws of energy and vibration, because you must understand simply and clearly the laws which govern the world of substance and energy in this universe. These laws are very simple and are very clear. When properly understood, an individual in the knowledge of his own I AM Presence is able to command with authority everywhere he moves in the universe. Energy, Matter, Vibration are all one. Love is the word we have chosen to signify all things, that is, Energy, Matter, Vibration. When an individual understands the word "Love" he understands the word "God," for God is Love. Understanding these words, blessed ones, is not merely a mental comprehension of the abstract idea behind the words. True understanding of words which contain such significance and power can only come with the heart lifted and the eyes raised in gratitude and aboration to the One, the Great I AM Presence of the Universe.

So many times earnest and sincere students of Light misunderstand the laws concerning energy and vibration, misunderstand them sometimes almost willfully, because of their intense desire to have a mystical experience, their

100

intense desire to have a demonstration. Beloved ones, our
proof is with you in your hearts, and the proof of the
reality of the Laws that We give you is in your everyday
life as you practice what We tell you.

The Laws of energy and vibration, while immutable,
are just and joyous laws. They bring no pain or suffering.
It is humanity's nature to try to make suffering out of
them. Humanity suffers because humanity does not like
certain human things and has not accepted the Divine
Law and the Divine Understanding, that is all. The
struggle which so many have experienced from time to
time has not come about because of God's Laws but has
come about instead because of humanity's inability to let
go of itself as humanity and accept itself as God.

Dear ones, the Laws of Love are the Law of Life. If
you understand the Laws of Love you will live forever.
There is no death, for Life and Love and God are one.
Therefore, in your understanding of these great Truths
you will go on, yes, even in these bodies if you wish, until
you have obtained for yourself complete mastery over
your world, complete dominion over all things finite and
infinite that come within your sphere of action.

Energy released, dear ones, is not wishful thinking—it
is not hope, prayer, decree. Energy released is energy
released! You cannot, I assure you, move mountains and
accomplish miracles by hoping that those mountains will
be moved or that those miracles will be accomplished.
No! But the mountains can be moved, yes! In the activity
of the I AM Presence there is a Reservoir of Energy more
powerful and more vast than all the physical strength,
than all the armies of the world rolled into one. Your call
to that Presence, your acceptance of the answer of the
Presence, leaves the door open for that energy to come
forth.

How does that energy come forth? Your functioning
at the human level cannot possibly force the energy to
flow from your Presence. If the full power of the
Presence were to be released through you at one moment,

there would be a bright flash of Light and little else. Talk about your atomic bombs! Then how is it possible for this Great Presence of Life, I AM, Almighty God in Action, to release this energy in such a tremendous amount that it will move a mountain or accomplish a miracle?

The *key*, the *secret word*, the understanding to this Great Law is in your heart. It is only in the heart that the desire of the individual can be made pure enough and unselfish enough for the Doorway to open and the Limitless Energy of God flow forth. This is what was meant by the ancients when they said: "You must have faith," because in their simplicity they could not conceive of a better way of explaining the natural action of Law that took place. I assure you, dear ones, that Faith is the answer, but an explanation of that Faith is the acceptance of God's Plan in a completely unselfish and detached manner on the part of the individual who calls forth God's Energy.

When you as an individual on the pathway to Mastery learn to open your heart to God-desire only, accept only the unselfish, the Pure, the Perfect Plan in your mind, and then turn to God, the Wholly Pure and Perfect reservoir of all perfect things, let Me assure you that the energy, that is the physical energy required to open that door and let the unlimited Divine Energy pour out, that physical energy is so small that none of you will feel any sense of strain by having released it.

That is one of the rules to the release of the energy directly from the Presence, yet it has been written and said to you, "I and the Presence are one." How then is that energy to be released through you, you might ask. Blessed ones, this can be done and you will find it within your power to accomplish physically and mentally tasks beyond your outer conception of your ability if you will acknowledge only in your hearts—purify that heart of yours—and be sure that the motive is clear, is clean, is pure. Be sure that that which you seek is Light, then roll up your sleeves and go to it! You will not accomplish your permanent Victory by refusing to do the work that has to be done physically. No! You will rise up above all physical effort when you have conquered all physical things, but not before. You will learn to love the work that you must do. You will love it so that you will master it, and as you master it, it will become your willing and obedient servant, and you, the master, can move on to conquer more inspiring tasks.

Fear no work! There is no task that you as a student of Life cannot perform. Have confidence in yourself and do not worry and fret concerning your motive once you know that you are right. Have the courage of your conviction and with it retain a sweetness, a divineness of disposition that will make it easy for others to work with you.

Blessed ones, when those who work under My direction are given the task of directing the growth of mighty trees in great forests, or great prairies of grass and flowers, they might say, if they did not know the Law, that every stone encountered was a problem; every ravine down which the water ran, an obstacle, and they might despair of the job and say: "What good does it do to grow all these beautiful and magnificent things upon the face of the earth? At what cost, at what energy all this is produced. It is not appreciated. Man only destroys it as quickly as he knows how—and they learn more about that every day." But We do not stop, We continue creating and bringing forth new beauty, new perfection, through all kinds of obstacles, if you wish to call them obstacles. But, dear ones, do you see, they are not obstacles, but all makes for one complete universal whole.

If you could hear you would hear the sound of growing things. And the things that do not seem to grow, such as rocks and the things that are still, also have their sound, and it is in perfect harmony with the things that grow. Where is the discord? There is none. Is there an obstacle or problem? No! So it is with you. You are expanding. The Light in your heart is going out and as it goes out it meets, say a tough old piece of granite on its way, charging happiness in the mind of some other human being. Do not worry. That one also has a purpose in being there and at the lower levels is in tune, to a degree at least, with the Infinite. Make sure that you also are in tune.

Let your motive be pure, your intention right. Serve well your heart and then turn to God, Who is within and above you, Who is tangible and Real and All-powerful, before Whom the universe bows, and say to that God: "O Beloved I AM, come forth, release into this situation Thy Pure Energy. Bring about Thy Perfection here," and let your own Love go forth as the Love of your Presence to accomplish that thing. Blessed ones, your joy, your release, your freedom will know no bounds. Then, I plead with you, do not fall into that trap—do not stand by waiting for a manifestation, for some sign, for proof—just accept that it is done, and it will be done far more fully than you dream.

Beloved students, Friends, with My Heart I enfold you and Bless you tonight and every night, tomorrow and every tomorrow, on and on. As you go forward, be happy. Walk firm in the Light. Look ever upward, and O dear ones, keep your hearts open that the energies which the Presence of Life, Almighty God, giveth to you can flow out to bless a hungry and a thirsty world.

All My Love and Blessings with you now and always. I thank you.

Blessed Lord Maha Chohan

O Blessed Lord, Maha Chohan,
Thy Mighty Power from the Sun
Flows through the trees, the hills, the flow'rs,
Each living thing thrills to Thy Pow'r of Love Divine!

All Nature doth exalt Thee!
Thy Majesty in ev'ry tree,
In mountains and great waterfalls,
Thy Life flows through each one, Belov'd Maha Chohan!

Maha Chohan! Great Lord Divine!
We call to Thee with Love
To Bless earth from above.
We call to Thee! Maha Chohan!
Let Thy Mighty Currents flood Nature anew!

We love Thee, little Beings of the Elements,
The gnomes and salamanders, sylphs and undines too.
O precious little Beings, come and serve with us,
As once you did in days long past, with Joy we call to you.

O let your love flow forth to bless mankind again —
Forgive men their unkindness; grateful they shall be.
We love you, little Beings, come and serve with us,
Together we will love and serve mankind 'til all are free.

O Blessed Lord, Maha Chohan,
Thy Mighty Power from the Sun
Flows through the trees, the hills, the flow'rs,
Each living thing thrills to Thy Pow'r of Love Divine!

All Nature doth exalt Thee!
Thy Majesty in ev'ry tree,
In mountains and great waterfalls,
Thy Life flows through each one, Belov'd Maha Chohan!

Maha Cohan!   Maha Chohan!
We love You, Maha Chohan!

—B.C.—

XI

TRUE SILENCE
by the Goddess of Wisdom.

In the action of Light which is sweeping America and the entire Earth, no permanent progress can be made without the full understanding of I AM, and that full understanding is explained perfectly by the Unfed Flame—Love, Wisdom, and Power. Love, without wisdom, turns the attention to the outer physical world. Wisdom, without power, is merely a quiescent pool which has no action; and Power, without love, is merely force, the power of will to bind others to your desire. Without the three forces blended in the Unfed Flame and acting together in Perfect Balance, the understanding of I AM is impossible and perfect balance cannot come forth.

Now that I am again serving the humanity of this Earth I wish you to feel free to call upon Me. Long ages ago you knew Me very well under another name. In My last embodiment I was born as a result of the action of Light between My Father, the Mighty Silent Watcher, and My Mother. Since that embodiment I maintained My existence in one body for age after age, until finally the Ascension was granted and I went forth a wholly Pure and Perfect Being.

Thoughout the ages men have turned to Me and

called for My action, but unfortunately, they have not called in Love, and I, who am the full Power of Wisdom, do not move into action unless Love is acting, for that would not be wisdom. For generation after generation and century after century men have swept the world for knowledge, which they called wisdom, but it is not wisdom. No matter where you turn you find knowledge, but the pure and steady pathway to Wisdom is through your I AM Presence and the feeling of Love released to bless mankind forever.

In the coming cycle you will find that there are many old concepts which have been yours in the immediate past which, as you go forward, you will have to free your consciousness from and dissolve in the Fire of Forgiveness, for it will no longer be the part of wisdom to use the words "blast," "annihilate," etc. The word "dissolve" is all right, but the words that carry the feeling that an individual is taking control over another individual will no longer be in use, for under this radiation that will not be the part of Wisdom, and that is why I am among you. The Fullness of My Light and Power shall blaze throughout the minds and hearts of everyone, and it is My Light which shall enter into the heart of every human being and cause it to expand and blaze that same Light into the mind. When that takes place the individual is Illumined.

My Light pours forth into the physical octave in its Mighty Golden Ray. It is, with the exception of the power of Love, the highest rate of vibration in the universe, for Wisdom, true Wisdom, is really Love in action.

Very soon, from the standpoint of the Arisen Masters, it will be possible for the new children being released into the physical octave to come forth fully grown as a result of the blending of rays from the parents, and physical contact of the lower nature will be unknown. That was the activity which brought Me into being in My last embodiment, for I never knew childhood, nor did I ever know how to be an adult, for I AM the same Eternal Truth for all time. I AM the Mighty Flame of Wisdom which, when called to, will burst into myriads of Light within your heart, piercing the cells of the brain and bringing Love and Light to all mankind.

Call to Me for the Illumination which you must have. Man's partial illumination has led to cunning, deceit, and intellectual scheming of every sort, but I AM the full illumination which banishes forever every dishonest, disloyal thing and brings the full Understanding of Life which is contained in the words "I AM."

Never tire of making your affirmations and I assure you that the use of affirmations is the most powerful way of bringing forth any precipitated substance. You must claim a thing before you can have it, and how can you claim it, how can you have it, unless you enter in and acknowledge your own I AM Presence as the Power of Light which acts within you! I plead with you, beloved students of Saint Germain's Great Light, give obedience to that Great Light which beats your heart, and as you give obedience you will have the Illumination which will erase all misconceptions from your mind and let you know the Reality of Life.

You have heard Saint Germain say that blasting was one action of the Law, and so indeed it is, and you have also heard Him tell you that blessing was the whole of the Law applied, and when you rise into the understanding which I am releasing to you, you will see that to bless a person, even though he be viciously inclined, is actually to blast him with Love, with kindness, for I assure you that the feeling world of a vicious individual, seething with destructive energy, cannot stand the Light which is released by anyone who will maintain a kindly, loving attitude. Turn your attention to the I AM Presence. Listen to the Voice of that Presence, and know that in the I AM consciousness all is Love, all is One, and all is the great Wisdom of Light blazing throughout all time, throughout all space, and bringing with it Happiness, Perfection and ever greater Glory.

Many students feel, since learning of the ascension, that they do not need to take care of the physical body because they are going to get rid of it. May I assure you that is a very serious misconception, that is not the case. The body of the individual is precious and the most beautiful, the most wonderful creation of Life. It is indeed the Temple of the Most High Living God and should always be clothed, clean, and protected, and blessed as such. To ignore it, feeling that you are going to get out of it sooner or later, is absolute misrepresentation in every way, a misconception which will bring tremendously direful results if continued. I assure you the goal of the individual is not to get out of his body, it is to do so much while he is in it that he does not have to, but can take the fulfillment of himself with him as he leaves.

Use the Fire of Forgiveness, but do not neglect soap and water too! Use the I AM Presence to make your body symmetrical and beautiful, but do not mistreat it or refuse to give it proper exercise, the proper amount of air, proper ventilation. If you do that surely your temple will go to ruin. You must remember to purify your feeling world, your mental world, and your physical world so that all three of those bodies vibrate in perfect harmony as one—the bringing of Balance through the application of Divine Wisdom.

Beloved ones, in all that you do, you will express the greatest wisdom if you remain silent in all things. Remember that the Golden Flame of Wisdom which is pictured as the center plume in the Unfed Flame, leans neither to the right nor to the left, but points Godward always to your own I AM Presence. Thus it is always Wisdom to look first to your Presence. Wisdom is the one thing required more than anything else in the affairs of mankind today. I mean, of course, true Wisdom, not merely knowledge or the accumulation of factual information from the outer standpoint, but rather the Divine Guiding Power of Light which flows into the mind to illumine it, to turn it unto the heights, and to carry it forward unto Victory after Victory of Light.

I have said that it is not the part of Wisdom to use the expression, "blast" or "annihilate," for in using those expressions you tune into the very activity which you yourself wish and are decreeing does not exist. Then if you do permit that activity to enter into your own expression, into your own consciousness, you make yourself a part of the very thing We are striving so earnestly to dispose of. You will see that although it is not wise to use those expressions, nor ever in your heart to wish for the destruction of any individual, still it is the definite part of Wisdom for you to take a strong, determined stand for those things which you know to be correct.

It is extremely imperative that students of the Light learn to stand strongly and unswervingly in the Light in perfect silence. Remember, the Flame of Wisdom points upwards, and is always perfectly silent. So many times individuals will have an inner desire to accomplish a certain thing. They will call to their Presence but their own intense desire to accomplish a given activity will blind them, or dull them as it were, to the answer from their Presence so that the warning from the Presence not to go ahead might actually be mistaken for a definite prompting to go ahead; and that one, in his enthusiasm would go forward to carry out his desire mistaking his own thrill in personal accomplishment for the release of Light from his God-self.

Know always that your I AM Presence does not make mistakes, it is only the human that does that. That is why it is so important for you to learn to call to the I AM Presence at all times and then to put aside all human desire, that the information, the prompting from your Presence, may come through without human qualification. If you will really learn to put your faith, your confidence, in your own God-self, then you will very quickly find that you cannot go wrong, nor will you. But if you persist in placing your confidence in things of the outer world, your confidence will be misplaced in every instance, as there is no thing in the outer world which has any permanent value. Those things of real value are always of the Inner. They are those so-called intangible traits of mankind, the qualities of the Arisen Masters released into physical use which are the permanent cornerstone of the race and without which a civilization could not be. In the maintaining of those qualities of Godliness it is imperative that you stand for those qualities with all your energy. When you observe a brother or a sister about to perform an error, it is your privilege to call to their Presence that that error be not permitted. However, it is never wise to let the other one know that you are making that call.

My blessed ones, I assure you that perhaps the most important single step upon your pathway is the learning of silence. You must master your tongue, for it is those things which flow from your tongue when it is uncontrolled that you pay for most heavily. Learn to take your attention off the seeming appearance. Silence your outer self and go on with your confidence in the hands of God. Accept your oneness with the Divinity and let the Divine Wisdom of the I AM fill your mind, your being, with its own Golden Light Substance.

You must learn to be silent. You must learn not to discuss the laws which you know with those who do not believe. You must learn instead to apply the Law which you know, which will make you master of the situation and make it possible for others to wish to become like you.

Joy is a mighty motor, and with Happiness in action all things are possible. Realizing, as I am sure you do, that Happiness is the highest rate of vibratory action in the universe if it is that certain form which comes from pure Love, you will quickly see that when Happiness is in action all things are possible and you are at-one with all of God, or all of Good that is in action elsewhere in the universe.

Since consciousness is a universal quality filling all space, and since self-conscious individuals are focuses of the same consciousness drawn into physical manifestation, then you will be able to perceive that the highest and the lowest, the whole or in part are yet one, for all are consciousness. Since that is true, is it not the part of Wisdom to dwell in the highest state of consciousness where all things can be done?

Do not, I pray you, permit yourself to become disgruntled even for a few moments. It is a very simple matter when you are tired or when you do not have everything going according to the plan you have made, to let the feelings get away from your control, and these feelings are very apt to cause you to release energy misqualified, or cause you to release thoughts and words into action which definitely create and remain in action to perform their destructive work, until the Fire of Forgiveness has been used in its full power. I assure you, beloved ones, there is nothing more important than the learning of silence, not only of the spoken word but of the thoughts and feelings as well, for when you have learned to silence yourself in every way, then you are truly ready to go forward.

Mankind in its activity through the ages has, from the human standpoint, deliberately turned aside from God, the One Great I AM Presence—has deliberately set the law into action whereby the attention is turned upon outer things instead of the Source of all Good. You will see that the consciousness must reverse and the divinity within each one be given an opportunity to burst through like a Mighty Flame of Light. Then do you not see that before that turnabout can be made it is essential that the practice in the wrong direction be stopped before progress in the right direction can be begun. At that point of stopping is the great danger for then it is that all things

rise to the surface, but if the individual upon the
Conscious Pathway will always hold the attention upon
the Presence and upon Us, Who in Our humble way assist
mankind, then you will quickly see that though all
destructive things in the universe rise to the surface still
you need not be affected; but in the Silence you will
gather the strength which will cause you to turn about
and retrace your steps, going back to your own Great
Source of Life, the Infinity of Cosmic Consciousness,
which is contained in the very simple yet all-sufficient
statement "I AM."

Speaking of Wisdom, I assure you that one of the
highest courses of action for anyone today is a great
release of Love and Loyalty to his Country if he
fortunately finds himself an American. I stand with you
and say: "I Love you America, and I long for that day
when you shall be set free from bondage and the Divine
Heritage of the Cosmic Light itself shall be yours." I
thank you.

XII

YOUR POWER TO CREATE

by the Venetian.

The first step upon the pathway of the sincere student is the turning of his attention to his I AM Presence, and the second step is the anchoring of himself to one who will assist in going before him to make the way easy.

At all times since the unfoldment of civilization upon this planet there have been those who carried the Light, and there have been those who sought the Light. The ones who sought, after learning the source of Light, turned to the ones who carried, and as there are always fewer of the latter, one usually found small groups forming, different churches, different philosophies, different creeds.

The expression of any activity and the sustaining power of that activity has always been determined by the Light of the one establishing the activity and how well he has been able to draw to himself others who also could carry the Light. And therein you may find your first lesson, for the one who carries the Light must always be humble; must always be true to his own source, which will permit him to recognize the true worth of each one who comes to him. The one who is the greatest among you will be the one who will be the most willing to step aside that another who has perhaps partial greatness may express that which he has. If one has certain great qualities and with those qualities goes a pride of ownership, the pride will become greater than the qualities for good and the result will be disaster. Those who teach this Law should always bear in mind that when they say "I AM that I AM" they have voiced for all mankind the Eternal Decree which each one must learn to make. Knowing that all is one, that comprehension is easily attained.

Now comes the second rule, and this is perhaps as difficult in appearance from the outer as the first, in fact, many have felt that it was more difficult. When you observe a loved one, an acquaintance, or even a stranger about to make what is termed an error, about to go against the Law of the One, the law of his being, do not interfere. *Do not interfere!* The Master radiates Encouragement, Love, Kindness, and God-desire to the individual, but does not interfere; so must you also as you go forward upon the pathway. If a brother or sister willfully goes forward to make a mistake, the mistake lies in his or her own world and will be handled most quickly if no interference is given. Your obligation, as a student of Light, is to make the call to your I AM Presence, which is one with the Presence of the individual about to make the error, and release such a feeling of Divine Love and blessing that the error will not take place. Then, in connection with this, even though that one goes willfully ahead and commits the error, do not think less of him for that. Your feeling should not change.

And therein lies the next point of Law, for in your dealings with one another, if you persist in changing, saying, "This one I can love more than this one because the former is expressing more of God's qualities," then you are robbing yourself and the latter one of a mutual blessing, for you who have come consciously upon the pathway are obligated not only to love those who appear to be deserving of your love, but to love intensely more those who can be aided by your love. Upon the pathway of life you are actually upon the pathway of service, service first to your own I AM Presence always, and then service to mankind, for humanity is the reflection, the outpouring, as it were, of the Divine. Your obligation is to expand that Divinity within each one.

Think well before you speak, for idle words make up a tremendous sum of misery for the human race. Before making any statement you should consider well what its effect will be upon those who hear it and upon yourself, and if you would speak only as though you spoke in the presence of every human being in the world, only as though you spoke in the presence of the Arisen Host itself, only then will your speech be God speech and the I AM words flow through you with Full Power. "I AM" is your right to create, your power to create, indeed, you cannot stop creating, for "I AM" is you. Recognizing that as the fullness of the Divinity, the Three in One, you can move forward creating only Good, for only from God does created Good come.

This does not mean that you should be long-faced, sullen, silent, morose, and bad company. On the contrary, you should be joyous, carefree, deeply loving individuals. But may I caution you, when you enter into a very joyous feeling of laughter, of humor and good fellowship, be so careful that you do not with that laughter begin to feel superior, for with that feeling of superiority you elevate the human, which will instantly turn and cut another cruelly with a laugh, a word, a glance or a gesture. Even in your fun, be careful, and you will have more real fun than ever. Remember, slurring remarks in jest have a far greater power than a slurring remark not made in jest, for it is released with God's own energy of happiness. Be careful there, for the natural mirth and joy which man should maintain can be, unless controlled, an open doorway to many destructive things.

Speak clearly and distinctly, also. If what you have to say is worth the saying, then speak it forth that all may hear. If what you have to say is not for the ears of everyone present, do not speak it or imply it, and certainly do not whisper about it, or converse in a language not familiar to the majority of those in your presence. Instead, if you will train yourself to enter into the oneness of which you are a part, you will find you can communicate silently with anyone, conveying to that one only that which you wish that one to have.

In your conversation with one another, treat each one as an Arisen Master. How do you know but what each newcomer that you meet is an Arisen Master? I believe I may tell you something quite startling. There are a number of students who in the past have shaken hands with Arisen Masters and not known it. If you will begin to anticipate the tangible presence of the Arisen Master, your humble anticipation of quiet joy in his presence will bring Him to you.

To go on, may I say this: In your dealing with one another you have been trained by experience and by instruction which has been given to you in many channels and through long centuries. This training is making you more and more alert, more and more sensitive, more and more on guard, and for those qualities We greatly rejoice. How valuable those qualities will be when the student has learned to discipline himself that he be alert, on guard, and sensitive to the best within each one with whom he comes in contact, rather than the worst. When you meet one who is apparently suffering from some human habit and having much to handle, you will find that if you are alert you will be able to tell not the weak point but the strong point of that one. Then, by turning your attention and gaining the attention of the one upon that strong point, you will intensify it, and the weak point will become weaker and will eventually disappear.

Remember, beloved ones, everyone you contact is upon the pathway. Some, a very few, are consciously so, but regardless of their place upon the pathway, still are they upon it. When you help them you help yourself, for are not all things one? And as you call forth a blessing to your brother does not better than sixty percent of that energy remain to act in your own world to intensify the very thing within you which you called forth in your brother? Do you see why it is never wise to blast, to curse, or to condemn, for even though that which you blast, curse or condemn appears to need that type of thing, still do you intensify that same action in your own world, for sixty percent of that which you send forth remains to act within you—better than sixty percent. Do you begin to see the frightful consequences of that simple yet far-reaching misunderstanding? It does not take a Master to destroy. Remember that!

It takes a master craftsman to build a watch, yet a careless child may destroy that watch in a moment, but can the child rebuild it? No! So it is with individuals; so it is with nations. It is easy to destroy; it is the pathway of least resistance. Those who consciously go forth upon the path to mastery build always. They build, not for themselves selfishly, but for others, and that generosity of assistance to others builds most firmly for themselves.

I have observed many misunderstandings rising among those who consciously serve the Light, and one of the most painful of those is the misunderstanding that in order for an individual to make progress he or she must have a divorce, severing all ties that bind one to another in the human octave. True, any human tie that binds is a limiting, controlling activity of the human, yet do I say to you, enough Light called forth from the I AM Presence will change those ties that bind into a great outpouring of *divine* Love and blessing to each one. Beloved people contemplating separation should think well upon the Oneness of all things. How can the Great White Brotherhood expand itself by raising mankind into Itself unless it is a Brotherhood, a plane where all beings work together in service for everyone?

Returning again to the activity of speech with one another, remember always, when someone speaks to you, no matter what he says, he loves you. Even though his speech be to curse, still he could not curse unless love were there. If you will recognize the love within each one and intensify that by the Power of Light which you know and understand, by the focus of attention upon the I AM Presence, by the visualizing of the Flame in Action, then cursing will disappear and even one with termendously vicious intent to you will stop still in his path and hold his tongue.

You have been taught also, that to be still is to be very wise. Yes, that is true, for in the Silence true Wisdom comes, that is, the *true silence;* the true silence being that stillness in which the individual turns to his own Great Presence and commands Love to flow forth. But beware of the silence that is merely disinterest! Beware of the silence that is brought about by a sense of false security! Beware of the silence that plans in the dark! First you Know. Knowing, you must Dare. Daring, you must Do, and in the Doing you must be Silent!

Let Me say this to you also about giving. Do not hesitate to give. The I AM Presence did not hesitate to create your body. It gave it to you that you might give more Light in a darkened world. That Light may take many shapes, many forms, but your obligation to your Presence is to give all things which you have, and the one who will do that freely will sit upon a throne of Joy and Happiness sustained, and will never lack for any good thing. Yet, if that one in all his giving will not give until a price has been arranged for, then that one is not giving, he is bargaining only and the bargain that he makes will be his throne and will be but temporary, for his power to make good bargains for himself will diminish with the more bargains he attempts to make. Instead, let that one who has Light in any capacity ask how he may give it freely, never thrusting it upon any but only when he observes that the requirement is there, then let him step forth freely to fill the need. Such an one, moving in Love, may pass unharmed through any nation, through any group of people, through any situation, for all who know him will love him.

Seek not to better your position at the expense of another. If you would better your position, see what more you can give of yourself, of your Light. Give always! Give before you are asked, but give also after you are asked. And do not begrudge a gift thinking that it might be charity, for that is to say that your friend who loves you enough to give to you perhaps is only striving to make a bargain with you. Rather judge it by the *feeling* that accompanies it, and then when you have determined that, judge not at all, but bless the one who gives it without ceasing, and accept it wholeheartedly, whether it be given to you by one who has much worldly goods or by one who has apparently nothing. Rejoice that the way has opened for your brother, and then go on your way rejoicing still.

Remember, because this Power of Light which you understand and are beginning to apply does make you superior to your fellow beings in many respects, those respects are only from the appearance world, and there is no one anywhere who can say "I am more holy than thou." Therefore, when you observe a brother or sister not yet upon the conscious pathway, you, having applied the Law, having more than that brother or sister, do not proudly display yourself as being the one who has, whereas the other is the one who has not. Rather give praise and thanks that humbly it is your privilege to show the other how he too may achieve. Take no credit for it. No credit belongs to you. Give to your I AM Presence the recognition for all things. Remember that it is the part of Wisdom, the part of Mastery, to *do* in silence!

If you will live with the consciousness that "I AM all things which I wish to be," you will live in Harmony and Peace among mankind and yet you will be such a Conscious Power wherever you may be that you will constantly raise others by their desire to share your Love.

Love *freely* I plead with you, and by that I do not mean free love, but rather, calling the I AM Presence to release Its Limitless Outpouring to everyone. Stand by that! One million in America today who would do that together, even for five minutes, would change the world. That is the great requirement today.

*   *   *

Out of the Fullness of My great Treasure House I flow forth into the hearts and minds of mankind, filling them with Love, with Light, with Joy, with the Opulence never ending, for I AM All Things—I AM that Power of Light released. O Thou Wondrous Presence of Life, Thou All-powerful I AM, we acknowledge Thee in the hearts and minds and lives of everyone everywhere. We know that there is only God, Good, acting within each one. Recognizing that, we are at Peace and all discord ceases to be.

XIII

YOU ARE THE I AM PRESENCE

by various Masters

The Great Presence of Life, I AM, is Supreme! You as the individualized Flame of Life, the Great Presence Itself, must acknowledge your own Source, your own Oneness, your own ability to create, if we are to bring forth upon this planet any semblance of Peace and Order.

There pours into your body, into your world, a stream of energy which beats your heart and sends the blood coursing through the veins which makes life possible. Do you not see that it is impossible to accept lack when you realize that the Life which is surging in and through you at all times is God in Action? You are at-one with that Creator. It is the energy which you use when you breathe or raise your hand. Do you not see how it is impossible for you to lack for courage, confidence, strength or energy? Never accept for a moment that you do not have the full Power of Light and Love surging through you now and always, and through mankind who are working with you learning these mighty Laws.

God is real! God is your heart, your life, and fills your world at each moment, taking you onward and ever upward, if you but choose to go. This Great Presence of

Life, the I AM of you, is individualized for you, and yet at one and the same time, is the same Presence that governs every other individualized focus upon this planet and throughout all Infinity. There is only one God! There is only one Light! I AM is that one. Acknowledging yourself to be at-one with this great Truth will quickly clear away the fear that has blinded you in the past.

It makes no difference what you have studied—indeed it makes no difference what you know—until you acknowledge yourself as being one with the Eternal Quenchless Flame of Life, the I AM Presence, you have not begun to make your own eternal progress. But from the moment that you do take that step, you can never turn aside permanently, for you are the Life, you are the Light, for the Arisen Masters' Law which is hereby given to you is the Light of the World. Turn to the Presence for guidance. Make every moment a period of contact with the Great Inner Force that beats your heart!

Love first the Great Presence of God in you individualized, the Great Almighty Source of Life, Recognize your own divinity. Recognize your responsibility as that divinity *to act* and bring Perfection into your world. Hold all with whom you come in contact in perfection. Let that perfection flow forth from you that all with whom you come in contact feel that perfection. Then, when you have loved the Light that beats your heart, love all of God's creation everywhere.

Never fear and never hesitate! Call your Presence into action, sweeping and surging through you, bringing you Peace and Power and Perfection, and raising you. These things are *real!* These things are *true!* Accept the great Reality of Life here before you each instant. Acknowledge it! Expand it! So that mankind will understand and join hands with you, going forward into the Perfection of the age to come.

Never doubt for one moment the reality of I AM. Never doubt it, for that Great Presence which beats your heart is the All-enfolding Limitless Presence of God.

There is nothing more magnificent—there is nothing more pure—nothing more glorious than the activity of the students in turning their hearts and minds to that Great Presence, accepting by so doing the connection between themselves and God. *Feel* and *accept* that mighty coursing Energy of Light flowing in and through your heart.

Feel! Accept! Apply these laws! Accept the Consciousness of your I AM Presence emblazoned in your mind. Feel! Accept the Power of the Fire of Forgiveness!

As humanity learns more about itself it must learn that sooner or later it comes face to face with the inescapable fact that humanity exists in direct relation to God; that His Power moves through each one, giving Life to the body; and when humanity will recognize that, and that the individual has dominion over that Light, then and then only will he move forward to Mastery.

The Miracle of Life dwells in your heart, if you care to observe it. The Miracle of Life dwells in your heart— the greatest Miracle that has ever taken place. Call the Miracle Working Presence into action, for it is up to you to make the call that you will accept the Miracle of the Christ within yourself. You are living proof of that reality, for all that matters is you.

The I AM Presence is the Living God, the Full Power of Life in Action for you, which will surge through you at any time, *instantly*, to give you protection, assistance, or direction. Live as conscious of your I AM Presence as you are of any part of your physical body, and blessed ones, become as conscious of the presence of the Arisen Host as you are of the presence of physical beings about you. Learn to accept the reality of the things you do not see, that you may receive the most powerful benefit from those unseen forces, which are the most powerful in the universe.

Up through the ages this instruction has been given to mankind. A few gathered in one place, an individual watched and guarded in a far corner of the Earth, slowly, painfully taking many, many years, individuals were trained, directed, raised, illumined, and today these same individuals are the Wayshowers for the race.

When you hear the words of the Presence speaking in your heart, you know that you also have chosen. This is your call, and you may answer it by calling aloud to your own Presence, your own individualized I AM self. Only thus can you make progress. Only thus can you rise above the binding chains of limitation, of human discord, of apathy, delay and disintegration. Only thus can you don the Eternal Robe of Light, forever put aside the enemy called death, and walk through those Eternal Halls of Light, and walk as Gods among mankind.

Those who choose to follow those who have gone on ahead, let them come after. Let them look neither to the left nor to the right, but only forward, upward to the Light. Let them sing the song of Love which lasts eternally and fills all space with its pure beauty. Let them be unafraid, but onward, praising, onward let them say:

"MASTER, WHAT MORE CAN I DO?"

* * *

The I AM Presence is the goal for every individual and as you turn your attention to that Presence *within and above* you, turn your energy back to that Source of Life, you will have entered into that activity which will take you forward into your great Eternal Victory. What a magnificent thing to understand! Never tire of thinking of your I AM Presence. Never cease to call for It to bless others. Never cease your outpouring of joy that at last the full truth has been revealed.

Accept the Presence in everything that you do. In every activity that you set out to accomplish, before you start observe the Presence resting over it and see blazing through it the Light of the Electronic Body of your God-self. Every individual you observe, see him through the shining White Light of the Purity of your Presence and know that God is acting in that individual. Every condition you observe, see it through the gigantic activity of Life, the Great I AM, and know that perfection is coming forth.

Know always the I AM Presence is the instantaneous solution to all things. Notice, I have said, "the instantaneous solution." In the I AM Presence all things become One. There is no time or space, and when you make the call for any perfect condition to come forth, know that it is done. Do not question any longer, just accept, and go forward, giving praise and thanks that the I AM is the Great Loving Principle, the Great Ruling Power of all Life.

Make your I AM Presence the center of your world in your human self. Keep yourself balanced, but remember that *the Presence is the hub of the Universe,* the Central Point from whence all life flows. Is it not magnificent to realize that the Great Wondrous Presence contains the full Power of the Universe, and will release it into your use!

There is no death! Life is Eternal, and Life and God are One with you, for *you are the I AM Presence,* the I AM that I AM, the Presence of Life everywhere forever! You are that Presence, the very *essence of life* which flows through your feeling world and then flows on to bless, to heal, to strengthen, to inspire. *You are the Light!* Before the Dazzling Brightness of your Inner Self all darkness flees. *You are the Christ,* the only begotten Son of your own God-self. *You are the Eternal One, the Quenchless Flame, the Everlasting Sun!* You are all things!

Now feel those same statements and accept them as you say: "I AM all things that I wish to be. I AM my Life, my Joy, my Love." O blessed ones, do you not see how real, how tangible, how practical all this is? Will you

not accept that it is not so much what you *do* but what
you are *within* that matters?

The words "I AM" not only are the great Creative
Words, but represent, when completely understood, the
sum total of man's wisdom upon this planet. Through the
use of those words your Freedom and Victory are
attained. The misconceptions which have crept in
concerning the use of those words are of very serious
nature and have come about because of the desire of the
outer, the human self, for recognition, for profit, or for
some other human thing.

There is nothing more important, there is no single
thing of greater magnitude than the stilling of oneself and
the knowing, the consciously accepting of the fact that
the I AM Presence is within you, is your individualized
source of God in action. That is the supreme knowledge
which has been released, and when humanity recognizes
and accepts that, and that when they ask, they shall
receive, they will learn and know that the Glory of God is
very real.

Remember always that your password into or out of
any activity or situation is always the same, regardless of
the point of attainment you have reached. This password
is "I AM" and as you understand the fullness of the
meaning of those words you will raise yourself in
consciousness until all things are open to you, all points
anywhere in the universe may be visited by you freely
and at will, and will obey your own behest of Love, and
your world will be in Divine Order as you fully
comprehend the meaning of those great words—"I AM."
Do not at any time use those words lightly or
promiscuously, but forever guard your speech!

Accept your full authority, your God Dominion, and
grasp that Scepter of Dominion firmly in your hand and
move forward commanding all outer things into
obedience. Know that as you speak the Word, the I AM,
all things must come into Divine Order. Accept that and
recognize that God-power within you. See nothing else;

know nothing else; accept nothing else! Know the I AM of you is the Eternal, the Everlasting, the All-enfolding Flame of Life which is one with all things, the Infinite, the Eternal.

Accept the full Power of Life as it flows through you flooding your world with the fullness of all things. Know that your Presence is at the same level as the Presence of the Great Ones, and in that you stand at-one with the Arisen Masters' Consciousness.

Your I AM Presence is not concerned with personalities or creating impressions. It is not concerned with people's feelings. It is the absolute Law.

Your heart, which is the anchoring place of the I AM, will tell you what the perfect thing for you shall be. Know always that as you turn to that Presence and accept Its Blazing Light, Its Mighty Omnipresent Reality, you have entered the Realm of the Arisen Masters and stand at-one with the Great God Presence of Life, the I AM.

The time is here when humanity must take its stand! Mankind must determine individually and collectively to refuse acceptance of those things which are less than the Perfect Plan of the Great Presence of Life. The Perfection of Life is self-apparent! The imperfection of human understanding is also self-apparent! The only way to raise the human understanding to a point where the Perfection of Life fills it is for that human understanding to increase in vibratory action to the point where the understanding ceases to be human and becomes Divine. This is a very simple matter for the trained student of Light. It is also very simple for anyone who is sincere and wishes to move forward constructively for the balance of his human experience.

Man must realize that he has come forth upon this planet to serve, to render a great service, and your own greatness will be determined by the extent of the service which you render. You as one individual will never be great, will never go forward to greater perfection until you have learned to silence your own desire and replace it with the desire to assist others.

There is no happiness ever found in your world until you have stopped considering your own human self! Even the temporary joys which you sometimes seek and find to be very bitter after you have apparently drained them to the dregs, even these temporary joys can never be yours until in some small measure you have attempted to give joy to some other. Life for the individual is life for all.

The disappointment and the sorrow which you may have experienced should be proof to you that when mankind suffers, so in like measure do you suffer. When man rejoices, so in like measure do you rejoice. With that understanding you will see that you as one individual are a part of the whole, and therefore, as a part of that whole you will reflect accurately the feeling of the whole. This is the Law of human accumulation.

Here is the Law of the Arisen Masters: You are not a part of the whole, *you are the I AM,* which is the whole. Therefore, you no longer reflect the condition of others, you as the I AM Presence create the perfect condition in your own world and in the world and affairs of others. You cease to be the individual acted upon and instead you become the all-powerful God Presence acting, commanding Divine Love, Divine Order, Harmony, and Perfection to fill your world and to flow forth to fill the world of others. This is the Arisen Masters' Law. This Law you as an individual must learn.

The simple process which will take you forward in your understanding of this magnificent truth is the learning of absolute self control. As long as you persist in letting your human self turn your attention one way and then another; as long as your feeling world is subject to fits of passion, anger, greed, envy, and other feelings which are less than perfection, so long do you trod the human pathway—so long do you refuse to master yourself and to gain your self control. You do not have to be a giant intellect to accomplish this control, for your intellect, regardless of its training, regardless of all past experience which you might or might not remember, is but as a grain of sand before the Light and Wisdom of Eternity which flows forth at your bidding from your own God Presence.

I cannot mention enough the imperative need of turning always to the Presence and becoming used to the fact that the I AM Presence is *within you* at all times, and that you have every right and every authority to turn to It at all times.

Make your application and be happy, be free. Stand supremely confident in that which you do, knowing that God, the I AM Presence, accepts no appearances, accepts no delay, accepts nothing but Perfection manifest now. And always in that Presence—"I AM the Conquering Presence moving forward and bringing about the perfect condition in my world at all times."

Remember that you are beings of Love; remember that you are beings of Joy; remember that you are beings of Victory! Your Love, your Joy, and your Victory will come about when you put your I AM Presence first and everything else second. The unfortunate thing which chains individuals to limitation is that instead of putting God, the I AM Presence, first, they persist in putting some human being first, and just so long as there is a false god in the way of love to the I AM Presence and the attention to the Presence, just so long will that individual be unable to control his thoughts and feelings, will be unable to gain his own mastery, you may be sure.

In making the call to the Presence naturally the Presence can handle everything. The Presence is the All-knowing, All-seeing, All-thinking Light of God that Never Fails; but remember, *you* are the Presence! The Presence will release to you Life without ceasing, for *It is Life*, and you are your own Life. The Presence will see to it that your life is used to expand perfection if you use the desire to do that, but the desire has to be within you.

Now do you see why it is absolutely imperative that if you wish to make progress you not only have to make the call to your Presence, but you have to be prepared to release sufficient energy that the Presence may fulfill the call. That is all a matter of energy and vibration.

As it has been said, "virtue is its own reward." When you as an individual live the Law of Love, the Law of Life, turn your attention to the I AM Presence and the Great Beings who stand ever ready to assist you, you do not need to have proof of the reality of that Presence or the Great Ones, for the proof is instantly in your own world as a result of the radiation, as a result of the action which you automatically will have and experience.

Hear My Voice, My Child, My Son of Light. Listen and believe, for the Voice of God has always spoken through man. The way is now open for those who really want the Light. Rejoice and sing a great song! Lift up your hearts, your heads, your hands, and be at Peace. Know that the Great Host of Light which has guarded and directed the destinies of men still guards and directs them, and THE LIGHT OF GOD NEVER FAILS!

XIV

LOVE

by Sanat Kumara.

Children of Earth, this planet has been held in chains of bondage for centuries and now at last after fierce and pitiful struggle, these chains are being dissolved by the Light of the Arisen Host. That Light works through every individual who prepares himself in any way to be a channel for the outpouring.

My precious children, will you remember to follow the Laws of the Arisen Masters, and will you forever challenge the human? Remember, dear ones, if We give you a Law We do not at the same time give power to an individual to enforce that law through you. I mention this particularly because of the words which have just been read to you concerning hypnotism. Do you not see that with the clear definite explanation of hypnotism before you, if the explanation were followed and the law there given obeyed, those thousands of students which are now held under the hypnotic control of one individual would be set free; but instead those precious ones are convinced by hypnotic suggestion that anyone who could give them the law of hypnotism would not think of using the law against them. You see how sinister forces can be and how cunningly they may reverse

themselves unknown to the outer standpoint and bind
you upon the rack of indecision, inharmony, and failure.

Precious ones, I bring you Freedom—the Freedom
from old chains and bondages—the Freedom of Light,
which is yours for the asking, yours for the taking. No
human being or group of them may control God's Mighty
Power! You, as one individual, are of as much importance
to the Presence, that Great Omnipresent One, as is any
other one.

One of the most amazing traits of the humanity of
this planet has been their refusal to accept the oneness
between themselves and their Presence, the Great I AM.
Instead of doing this they constantly strive to take God's
Wisdom, Light, and Energy, claim it as their own and
then become the lords of creation without recognizing
the real Divinity, the real Godhead. Blessed ones, the
information concerning changes due upon this planet
have been given you for your freedom and blessing.
Beware of those who feel that because of their knowledge
it would be a most divine thing for the cataclysm to come
swiftly. I wish you to know, dear ones, that the
accomplishment which We hoped to make was achieved,
and come what may upon this planet now, the Forces of
Light shall win! Therefore, We rejoice! We rejoice
exceedingly!

Blessed ones, in your position you may not yet
rejoice for from your standpoint the battle is not won,
but We who see its outcome urge you on to every effort.
There are qualities which have been released into your
worlds and others which will be given to you that will
make you impervious to much that comes your way if
you will accept these qualities in action in your worlds.
The work to be done in this coming cycle will depend
largely upon Earth's children who have great courage
and who dare to do the right thing even though they fly
in the face of grave danger. The raising of the vibratory
action of this planet, or the evolving of it from the lower
into the higher realms, has brought forth now embodied

magnificent men and women who, when they understand these simple Laws will apply themselves swiftly, and their magnificent accomplishment will stand for ages.

There is one certain cure for any mishap; there is one certain action which will take you swiftly through any and every darkness—that is Love. *You must learn to Love,* blessed ones. You understand that action so little as yet. You must learn to Love, for *Love is giving.* You must love humanity until you give yourself to humanity. You must love the Truth until you give yourself for the Truth. You must love those things which you attempt to do so much that you give yourself to those things, for I say to you, those things that you truly Love you do not seek to have but rather to use for the benefit of all, that you may give of yourself in greater abundance, asking never for any compensation.

Children of the Light, stand together! Move arm in arm and hand in hand. Let your concern for one another be raised into the vibratory action of Pure Love. Let your desire to direct the destinies of others be raised into the activity of Pure Love, for in that holy realm of Light where Love, Pure Love, is the only motive, Peace and Joy will remain Supreme and yours will be the Victory. Know at all times:

I AM the Commander of my own destiny.

I AM the Conquering Presence which fills my world with the assurance of my I AM self.

I AM the Voice of God speaking through God's lips.

I AM the humble, calm, beautiful, magnificent child of Light.

I AM able now to bring forth every Good and Perfect thing that I require.

I now accept my oneness with that of the I AM Presence, and accepting that oneness, I move forward to be the fulfillment of my every decree.

May you always feel the Light, the Love, and the Blessings flowing from Us to you. We are those, We

Kumaras, who came originally from Venus, and with this New Cycle these two planets now become one. Do not imagine for a moment that I mean that oneness will take place on the physical plane, but the way is now opening, blessed ones, for those great souls who have made much progress, to move consciously from this realm of Earth to the planet Venus and there consciously recall all their experiences and return again with the full memory.

XV

THAT PEACE MAY REIGN
by the Goddess of Peace.

O blessed ones, may I begin by asking you please never to try to deceive one another. There can be no Peace as long as there is a feeling or a desire to present something other than it really is. Precious children, for the sake of your own progress in the Light, for the sake of the great Victory that you are surely winning, stand guard over your thoughts and feelings. Remember that a thought and a feeling, although two activities, are in reality one; for while it is perfectly true that many thoughts, especially the abstract, have very little feeling in connection with them, still there is a small portion of it acting, and a feeling, even though you have not willfully called the feeling forth, has been preceded in some measure by a type of thought even though not necessarily a constructive thought or a perfectly comprehensible thought. The activity of thought and feeling, divided for your understanding, are in reality one. Therefore, you do not have to wonder what is acting, whether it is your thought that is wrong or your feeling; merely call on the Law of Forgiveness, asking that all things imperfect be taken from you, and go forward

137

accepting only perfection in your thought and feeling world.

Knowing that you have the instantaneous power to bring forth anything you desire, through your I AM Presence, should make you free and take you forward as Kings and Queens of the Earth. This must come forth, for you blessed ones are the only ones, the only Power that could ever rule the Earth. I am not referring now to this particular group, but to mankind everywhere. Mankind has been placed on the Earth as the ruling, the God Presence, to maintain order in all things, but unfortunately man has done just the opposite. He has misused his God power and brought about inharmony, discord and disintegration. Now it is your privilege, with Mine, to work together for Harmony, for the bringing again of Peace and Joy upon this planet.

From tonight on I shall take up My abode in this area. I shall use as My radiating center that portion of ground which you have used as Treasure Island; this is the real reason for which it came forth. That plot of ground will be called one day the "Island of Peace," and there will come to rise a statue of My likeness to stand as the twin focus with the Goddess of Liberty upon the eastern shore. Liberty and Peace shall be the Cosmic Mothers of America, and it is My great and humble privilege to come to you this night to begin that activity for America and the world.

O do not think, blessed ones, just because We are invisible to the outer physical sight We have no power to bring all things into Peace. I assure you We have All Power and All Dominion to do all that is necessary to assist in clearing men's minds of the discord, of clearing men's worlds of inharmony, greed, envy, and all the subtle sinister forces which would deprive men of their own freedom.

Precious ones, do not be alarmed if while I am speaking with you the vibratory action of the room increases and you feel many things come to the surface.

Please do not be alarmed or misqualify anything that takes place. Know that things will come into Divine Order. Naturally when you are in this powerful focus—and I assure you it is much more powerful than you dream—the things which are in your world, which are in your consciousness (for of course, your world is your consciousness) those things which are in your world will come to the surface and quickly intensify. That is why it is so greatly imperative that you stand guard over your thoughts and feelings; if there is a thought of imperfection it will intensify just as quickly as will a feeling of Divine Love.

You must realize you are dealing every minute, in the Arisen or unarisen state, with the Law of energy and vibration. You cannot avoid it, and We cannot. It is your great privilege to bring back that oneness again which you once had, that feeling that there is only Light and Love.

My precious children of Light, do not feel discouraged if you find that suddenly after you have made much tremendous application you find your feeling worlds disturbed. Do not be discouraged. Precious ones, do you not see that that feeling of discouragement is just what the sinister force wishes you to have? When you find that you have made an error, rejoice, not that the error has been made but that you know it was an error, and therefore will wisely in the future not make the same mistake again. Feel the power of Peace penetrate your worlds, filling them with Joy and Happiness. Until you have such Joy and Peace in your heart that you can approach the one human you think is your greatest enemy, put your arms about him and bless him with your love, until that time you will never know real Peace.

Right now, it is true, We are working day and night to set aside certain activities of the Great Law which, according to the vast accumulation, had to outpicture in violent struggle somewhere upon the earth. O be grateful, precious ones, that you live where you do, that your home is here in this Land of Liberty and Peace, in this Land of Freedom!

It is true that during your waking state you are called upon to render a service in the outer world to some who do not come to these classes, or you are called somewhere to render a brother or a sister assistance, but all this you do in the outer is as nothing as compared to the great service rendered by you when you go forth and leave these denser bodies at night and assist others of the human race. Do you not see that the actions of man in the world are but the outpicturing of the Inner world? Then when that world of cause is purified and is peaceful and harmonious, then the outer manifestation of the Inner realms will be something beautiful to behold; but you cannot with a poisonous seed bring forth something beautiful.

Please remove from your consciousness the idea of great numbers. Due to the activity of great numbers in other activities of Light you have the idea that you really can't do much until you become numerous. Don't you see that much which has caused the great delay in the expanding of this Light has been caused purely by the great numbers who came in with the desire, not to serve the Light but to profit in some small way or great way? Do you not see, dear ones, from Our standpoint We would rather have one individual who gives obedience to Us than a million who think that perhaps they might profit in some way by what We tell them. Do you not see that you must put aside all thought of self! Do you seek to use the Arisen Masters Laws to benefit yourself? Then watch and learn that that is not the Law of God, for the Great Cosmic Law that forever keeps Order throughout all space is that *you must not seek for yourself but for others.*

You must, of course, use your Higher Consciousness in discriminating between right and wrong, but blessed ones, you do not have to use your higher consciousness to discriminate between the ones you shall love and the ones you shall not love. There is no discrimination there, for your obligation as a child of Light is to Love all Children of Light. It is to love life wherever you find it no matter how it may appear to you, no matter how poorly it seems to outpicture, your obligation is to love that life for that life is you, God. While it is life individualized through another, it is still your own.

Dear ones, when you find your attention reverting to any one individual with the suggestion coming to you always that that individual irritates you, disturbs you, or makes you uncomfortable, when that comes to you, still your human self firmly and march straight over to that individual and tell that one that you are going to be at Peace, that you are going to pour forth Love, and that you will be the special friend of the one whom you think annoys you, and then give obedience to that.

Before you retire at night will you not follow this suggestion and keep at it. Do not do it just for now while I am here prompting you and then in a few days forget it. It would be well to write this down and have it handy for your constant use. When you retire at night send thoughts of Love and Blessing and feelings of Love and Blessings to everyone that you think irritates you, and remember that I say *feelings*. So many times I have watched precious ones from afar off and they have tried to give obedience to this request in this manner: They would say: "Beloved I AM Presence send that love to assist such-and-such a one, but for heaven's sake keep them out of my world." My precious ones, as long as there is a feeling of that sort you have not forgiven or forgotten, nor are you living the Law. When you call the action of the I AM Presence to send Its Love, send your own too that the Presence may act through you as well as for you, and see that you send a *feeling* of Love, which is really one with your thought, unless you wish to be a house divided against itself. If there is some individual who disturbs you, go out of your way to be kind and gentle to that one that you yourself may be master of your world and perhaps assist in helping the other to master his.

Dear ones, have you not learned yet that you are all One—all brothers and sisters united in the Great Presence of Life? Then how can you think for a moment that there is somebody some place that you cannot get along with? It may be there are some who will refuse to get along with you, but precious ones, you can still get along with them if you care to. Is it not amazing that the activity of war upon this planet has come forth solely because individuals have persisted in believing they could not get along with certain individuals. I tell you truly that you can get along with anyone if you desire to. Just think for a minute, if someone were to pay you ten dollars for every kind word that you said to an enemy, do you see how quickly he would become your friend, and you become quite wealthy too! Then instead of paltry temporary gain from the physical standpoint why not seek your Eternal Freedom by thinking the same thing?

Precious ones, our Great and Blessed Friend Who stands with Us and Who assists you so closely, once made a statment which I think it would be wise for you to remember at all times: "Love thine enemies." Think what that means, and when you really have the comprehension of that, the word "enemy" will disappear from your vocabulary.

The Way is now opening, My blessed ones, for your worlds to be filled with Happiness and Joy, with Peace and Love, such as you little dream possible. But never fear, that reward which I mention will come to you from your own God-self, your I AM Presence, which stands at the same level as the Arisen Masters and Great Cosmic Beings; and it will come to you through your own Presence by your own application, for these are laws and rewards We would love to hand to you on a golden platter, but you would not know how to use them until you yourself prepare the way by earning them. So let that golden platter that presents you with the Great

Powers of Life be the goal of application, of energy released, that presents to you now and forever all Good and Perfect things.

My Love enfolds you. My Strength upholds you. My Joy flows through you. I AM the Perfect Peace unfolding within your hearts. I thank you.

Great Goddess of Peace

The Call:
Great Goddess of Peace we call unto Thee!
We call, we call, we call!

Great Goddess of Peace, we call Thee,
To shower the earth with Thy Light,
That discord now forever cease,
And mankind dwell in Peace.
O Goddess Divine may Thy Essence Bright,
Thy Substance of Pure Crystal Light
Flow into the hearts of all mankind,
Forever to abide.

Great Goddess of Peace, we call unto Thee!
We call, we call, we call!

The Response:
My Peace enfold you, Children of Earth,
I AM a part of thy Cosmic Rebirth
Unfolding now in the hearts of men
Is My Pow'r of Peace, the Mighty I AM!
I AM the Presence of Peace!
I AM Its Enfolding Pow'r!
I AM the Voice in the hearts of men
Commanding Peace, be still —
Peace, Peace, be still!

—B.C.—

XVI

CLAIM YOUR GOD DOMINION
by Jesus.

From My Ruby Temple do I come to you this evening, My beloved children.

When the Great Central Sun, the Cosmic Light that governs this entire Universe, first decreed this planet Earth into existence, it came forth as a Blazing Sun of Light, glorious, radiant, a God Being, and upon it consciously impelled, came forth the individualized focuses of God's own Mighty Power. Each individual was fully aware of his Source, one with it, and able thus to live in a world of Love, expressing only Love. Having free will and seeking always to express greater love the individual's attention turned from his Source to other individuals, and then to other things, and each individual that should have been one with himself, began, oh through long periods of change, to manifest greater and greater imperfection.

The Great Cosmic Law, observing this, created the wheel of action and reaction, the wheel of reembodiment, upon which spins the developing ego for this planet. Onward and onward, through an endless chain of events the individual moves, and thus, through an endless chain of events has this great planet moved

145

also. Civilizations have risen and fallen. Empires have been built and collapsed. The Garden of Eden upon this planet was located originally right in your own beloved United States of America, for it is here that God's own individualization first came forth, and here only is the Doorway back into the Perfection, the Glory and the Beauty that was originally ordained.

Six great and mighty civilizations have ruled this Earth. The seventh is even now coming into being. It is the birth of the seventh that concerns you all at the moment, for it is through these terrific times that the Light of God must burst to awaken the Christ Light within each one. I AM the Christ Light within the heart of every man who cometh into this world. I AM the Flame Breath that enfolds all even unto Eternity. I am He who was with you and I am come again, for indeed I have never left you. Mankind has merely turned and wandered away from Me. *I* am real! I am far more than an empty symbol, than an idle dream. I am Jesus the Christ, and most of you here at one time professed to love Me.

If you will turn your attention within your hearts and become very still, it is possible for those of you who have advanced sufficiently now to observe the action of the cosmic screen as We portray certain events which are to come forth.

Behold, My children, the day of darkness long heralded upon this planet has come. The skies are overcast. Dark clouds envelop the earth. The forces of darkness wage a bitter war. Following the emblem of self-destruction they battle fiercely over land and sea and in the air, and even as they battle you observe the land shudders and heaves and portions of it sink beneath the billowing waves. Behold vast armies gathering from the remnants of these once mighty countries, surging now to bring destruction upon the land of Light, America. Inadequately prepared, not completely united, the forces of darkness seem about to overwhelm the Land of Light.

Great cataclysmic changes come. But do you see from the west of your great country moves the Legion, a Legion of Arisen Beings, swords in hand, who sweep before them all destructive forces; and the Light as of a Thousand Suns bursts forth, bathing this country from shore to shore. The angry waters of the oceans roll back and subside. New continents spring forth out of the depths, and here upon this Sacred Ground, America, begins the New Nation, the glorious Seventh Race, the final God-victorious race for mankind upon this Earth.

You, My precious ones, who are Children of the Light, you are the fathers and mothers of this race that is to be. Behold, and I will show you vast cities springing up, beautiful and glorious. Love, Honesty, and Purity as the keynotes, the Glory of God is now come forth to dwell upon the Earth. And thus My Kingdom is established, for I will come forth to rule all men, I and My Brothers with Me, working from the eternal Cities of Light, the Etheric Cities, and from the Great Temples which will be lowered into the physical octave, and will see all unite at last to bring this planet into its glorious position. This is the Great Cosmic Law.

My beloved ones, will you not claim the dominion that is yours? Will you not begin to sincerely manifest the Arisen Master qualities which you have and are? There is nothing for you to fear. If you will be strictly honest with yourselves and humble before this Mighty Light, all good things may yet be yours. Why do you hesitate when you have promptings which you should obey? Why are you caught so many times upon the wheel of indecision? Claim your God-given Dominion, your God-given Authority, and in the fullness of God's Love proceed upon your way. It is far better that you learn to *acknowledge the God in yourself* than any other single thing.

Knowing the changes that must come, it would be quite simple for one who looked to Me for help to say: "Well, what can I do? Would it not be better for me to step aside from my earthly occupation and merely stand by ready to give assistance?" I say to such a one: How can you give assistance if you are only standing by? Your Father, the I AM Presence, requires your service in *all* ways, always. Remember, all things belong to the Father, all things belong to your own I AM, for before you came forth in physical embodiment was still I AM, the Blazing Light of Love, the Perfection of all things. Then do you not see each of you has a mighty debt to pay, a debt of love to be repaid in Love? Knowing that, how wise is he who lives from his heart alone and gives back unto his Source all things which pass through his hands.

My beloved children, I am sure tonight you feel My reality, for you have all drawn very near to Me. I assure you the Arisen state, the Kingdom of Heaven, is the *only* reality, but your planet must outpicture that reality, and therefore are you in embodiment today.

Prepare, oh prepare, I plead with you, for that which has been termed the Day of Judgment is at hand. What is the Day of Judgment? It is the day in which Divine Justice acts instantaneously, for that which is sent forth is returned instantly to the sender, be it good or bad. Everything has been intensified to that time. Hold yourselves very harmonious and pour forth love. Thus and thus only will you assure yourselves of safety, of joy, of beauty, of supply during the coming days. Serve from morning 'til night, eagerly, constantly and then serve also from night until morning. Much is yet to be done. Your sincerity, your Love, will make all things possible.

On the Ascension

My precious ones, remember, life is eternal, life is real and everlasting. O there are so many who doubt My reality, and yet they would have the tangible proof if they would only prepare themselves for it. Mankind has so long doubted the reality of the ascension and instead turned its attention upon the crucifixion that today the vast armies of the world are bringing about the crucifixion of civilization, which you will see cannot be slain but will rise again into the perfect state, even as does each Arisen Master.

Precious ones, do you not see that as it is with the individual so is it with the nation, and thus is it with the world also, for the nation is really just a body of individuals and the world but a body of nations and thus, as it is with the one, so is it with the many, for all are really one. Thus the ascension of the individual is preparing the way for the ascension of the nation, and the ascension of the nation will raise the planet into the perfect activity of Light and Love forever.

Do not mistake me, dear ones, I am talking practical and truthful statements of life which you must understand. These things which I say are not in any way too spiritual or too deep for your complete comprehension. Precious ones, when will you understand that the great Victory of Life, the Ascension, stands before you, ever beckoning you onward—you cannot escape it. You prolong your earthly experience for a time, oh yes indeed—man has been doing that for thousands of years—but ultimately you must achieve the victory, for inasmuch as you have started on the pathway you cannot turn aside for long. Is it not beautiful and wonderful to know that the Victory of Light is certain for each and every child of God?

If your attention will only be turned to your Presence then you will feel the glory of life flow through your veins, coursing through your body, lifting and raising your consciousness, and bringing all into such perfect order forever. If your attention is divided into other channels you will have only partial victory, or no victory at all. Why then hesitate? Leap up with a mighty joy in your breast and sing that loud and glad song of creation! Know that life is ceaseless, eternal. Life is you, that Great I AM Presence of Life, and being one, there is no death, there is no limitation, there is no failure, for on and on you go into the Victory of all Victories!

Saint Germain has brought to you so clearly the law of the attention and the understanding with which you can train yourself to govern your thoughts and your feelings. Is it not a beautiful thing and is it not a wonderful thing that those laws have been given to you, and you cannot turn aside from them? O, there are many who doubt My reality and Saint Germain's reality, but there is no one who can doubt the reality of the Law that has been given.

So many times in the outer world there is the feeling of mankind, "Why should there be another than Jesus? Is not Jesus sufficient?" And there is even more often the cry, "There is nothing but God. Why should we have to understand or divide God in any way? Why should we have to understand that there are Masters? Of what value is that? Is not God enough?"

Dear ones, I assure you that the I AM Pressence is enough, and yet if you will not accept the manifestations of the Presence through the channels which have been prepared how can you have the fullness of the assistance which the I AM Presence is releasing to you constantly? I assure you, dear ones, in the victory which I was fortunate enough to attain please know that I did not do that of My own energy alone, for My Teacher and Friend, the Great Divine Director, prepared the way for Me, and He in turn was trained by another Blessed One, whom you also know, and so on and on we go. Thus, man is raised into the perfection of life. So, dear ones, when you deny Me, or when you deny Saint Germain, or when you deny any of the Great Ones, you merely deny the assistance which the Presence of Life has released for your blessing.

Why do you think I am arisen? Why do you think Saint Germain has made His Victory? Do you think it is for any selfish reason? If there were any selfishness left in Us there could not be the Mastery. We have completed the Victory that We could render the assistance to you. Is it not beautiful to know that the same victory stands before each one of you? Think what that means! I do not wish you now in thinking of the ascension to forget for a moment that you still abide in earthly forms and that your duty is still to your fellowmen. O no! The ascension is not possible unless you are rendering a service, unless you have learned to spread the Law where you abide at the present time.

You cannot rise above a condition unless you have proved yourself and the vibratory action of your being and world is higher and more intense than the condition in which you have previously manifested. Thus, through the purity of divine love you raise yourself, through the assistance of the Great Ones, into your original perfection of the Father's Kingdom—that Purity and Perfection which shall now fill the Earth.

Thus it is that you should always give praise and thanks for the assistance that comes to you for you know that Myself or any of the Great Ones may come at any moment. Sometimes We come as a friend you know, sometimes as a feeling directing currents of energy that you will be prompted to do the perfect thing, and sometime, when you have prepared yourself, you will see Us in Our tangible body, ever laboring to assist mankind. Then will your belief be complete and you will know the Great Victory of Life.

Do not lose courage. Do not lose faith. Things which you have called for shall be yours when Harmony and Love is complete enough. This time, dear ones, you will see the Glory of God upon Earth, for the day has come when mankind must turn aside from the purely intellectual and come into the pure life instead. Dear ones, I have taught the Law for hundreds upon hundreds of years and I tell you truly that unless you will love your neighbors, unless you will love those who stand near you, and especially unless you will love those who help you, you cannot be free.

Pour forth your love! Do not bind yourself—let your gifts of love pour forth in an unending stream. Speak from your heart that the purity of your love may never be contaminated by the thoughts of your intellect. Let your heart rule that you yourself may become king and master of all things. Learn the power of the attention, of studying and applying the laws which have been given. O dear ones, if you will only see that your thoughts and your feelings are the important thing and unless you govern them, then what can be governed?

For years now the children of Light turning their attention to the Presence and to the Great Ones have cried out so often: "O Saint Germain, O Jesus, let me see Thee that I may know Thy reality. O, if only I could see Them doubt would be removed." My dear ones, each of you has seen. Wherefore is the doubt? Today will be perhaps a marvelous manifestation for you, and yet tomorrow again will come the cry, "O, why cannot I see?" Each one of you has had the experience of Light and Love in your world. Why will you not remember? Each one of you has seen Me or another of the Great Ones. Yes, dear ones, you have. You have not always recognized, and you have rarely remembered, at least for longer than just a few moments, and yet you have seen Us in Our tangible forms. O you do not understand for the human intellect persists in saying, "All this is too wonderful to be true—all this is too marvelous to really happen," but it is not, it is so, dear ones. The Great Truth of Life is exemplified by the Arisen Host, and make no mistake about it, We are quite real, and We know full well what is needed and thus we release it to you.

In making your calls to your Presence remember to speak from your heart, that your love may flow forth and the release may come to you; and do not try to reason out these things, but continue in *knowing* that *God is real*. I do not ask that you have faith alone, but I do ask that you put your confidence, yes, your faith in the I AM Presence rather than in one another. Which one of you is more real and more strong than the Presence of all Life? Therefore do you see, give recognition and praise where it belongs. Turn your attention, turn your love to the Great Presence of Life, the Great I AM, and to the Host of Arisen Masters, that yours may be the perfect world in which to live. Feel the Love Flame, which is the true Fire of Creation, expand through your world. Know at all times that you have the Scepter of Dominion within you. You have only to speak in My Name, in the Name of Life, in the Name of Love, and all things shall be created and brought forth unto you.

In My ministry, which was really such a short while ago, although to some it seems as though it occurred many ages past, I spoke with such joy, and with such a love, and yet mankind immediately concluded that I was a man of sorrows and much suffering. Is it not marvelous what the human mind can do? Those who knew Me least concluded most. Is it not always the way? Those who refuse to look deeply into the problem or into the great Truth which they are endeavoring to learn will find that they know little of it, yet they are the ones who speak the loudest, they are the ones who always prate of what they know. Is it not amazing?

In the silence, My children, is the Great Wisdom. When you speak, speak from the heart and you will pour forth the Wisdom of the Silence. And do not think that the Arisen state is one of great sorrow, O no indeed! Here alone does the natural life of man take place. Here alone are We joyful and natural at all times. O precious ones, if you could only see and appreciate as I do how easy it is for you to attain your victory. Of course, it is always much easier to say that once We have accomplished it. You see the one who has made the accomplishment always knows that really it is quite simple.

The ascension is really quite simple and is only a natural activity of life, the fulfillment of all things. Do not think it is too difficult for you. Do not accept limitations in your world. Accept that you are here in physical embodiment now for the great purpose only to expand so much Light, so much Joy, so much Truth that the Earth cannot hold you and you will rise into that plane of activity where all individuals are perfect and where is the pure fulfillment of all things. Listen to the Voice of your Presence and be guided by the Truth and the Purity that is there.

Accept My Love and Blessings, which pour to you in an unending stream.

*   *   *   *

O Thou Majestic, Thou Radiant Sun of Life, We pour our unending Love and Gratitude to Thee. We accept Thy Power only, knowing that it is Light and Light alone that fills our worlds, that makes us breathe and have Our Beings, Our existence. Dear Presence of Life, I AM, let all quickly know the Joy and Beauty that is found within, in the Inner Realms of Light and Truth. Here do We abide. Here do We pour forth Our Love, and into this sacred spot must all mankind come when they have loved enough. O Thou All-enfolding Sun of Light, I AM the Father, I AM the Son, I AM the Whole I AM, the One.

XVII

THE TORCH OF LIGHT
by Godfre

Out of the fullness of Life, beloved children, I greet you in the name of the I AM Presence, that Great and Blessed Presence which you have come to know and which you have looked to with such Love and devotion. O if you could but see the Glories and the beauties in the Arisen state, I assure you, you would quickly put aside all human things and determine to discipline yourself to the utmost, to give every ounce of obedience necessary, so that the ascension would be yours in this embodiment. From the Arisen standpoint things happen much more rapidly than they do from the physical, and yet the day is not far away when you may well believe things are happening rapidly enough from the physical standpoint.

Beloved ones, I wish to point out certain things to you which, if you will give obedience to them, will make the way so much easier for you. Why, O why cannot humanity give the simple obedience necessary to these great Laws? Why must they always feel that the laws are coming from individuals rather than *through* individuals. As long as that feeling remains within an individual, then he will hold himself back from the progress which could be won. In the formation of any activity some one or

155

Some group has to head it, of course, even from the physical standpoint. Let us take for example a large corporation. A group of businessmen will get together and set up certain principles and laws to govern the activities of their business. If they are good businessmen, however, they do not think of it as their own activity, but a living, breathing entity of which all are a part; therefore, as they give their ideas and rules into it, the rules come through them, and as each gives obedience to them and each employee gives obedience to them, those rules will quickly come into action; and so it is with all life.

It is so amazing to see how precious, precious ones will get themselves all tied up in a knot over some trivial little detail that really has no sense whatsoever. O My dear people, mankind could be so happy, so radiantly joyous all the time, but these little tiny things come up and one individual will insist on trying to mind another individual's business! It is so amazing to see that when mankind has the Law, still it refuses to obey it, and the most amazing part of all is that the many who have the Law and know the most about it give the least obedience. O well, We will just be patient.

Now precious ones, in regard to the activity of your attention, let Me give you a little assistance. When you feel a great pressure coming upon you, please realize that that pressure is taking place in your mental or feeling world before it connects with your physical world. It has to, for in order to have contact with the physical world it must pass through the mental and feeling worlds. Now then, you have been told many times how your attention will open you to various suggestions and thought forms of the outer world, and you have also been told many times how if your feelings are uncontrolled, even for a moment, you open your feeling world to the more or less tramp feelings that exist in the outer world. You must realize then, since that is the case, that your attention, provided of course your feelings are harmonious and properly governed, will absolutely protect you. If you will use the Fire of Forgiveness, then the control of your attention will positively protect you against every condition, and even something that might arise in your own world could be very quickly dissolved. But so often, instead of calling for the Fire of Forgiveness and on the Law of Forgiveness, thus reversing the current, the student will promptly turn his attention to the condition, thus intensifying it, until he may be practically down on his knees yelling for help.

Whatever acts in your world is your fault! You are responsible for it. Whether an individual or a group of them sends something to you makes no difference to you. There has to be some corresponding fault within you or it could not act. My dear precious ones, do you think if somebody sent a vicious thing to Me now that it would have any effect upon Me? Why of course not! But that is because there can be no imperfection acting in My world any longer, so the force which they would send, although it might be a tangible force, would have no power to act in My world, for there is nothing in My world that would correspond to it in any way. That is the condition you must begin bringing to yourself, and as you begin being generous with one another, giving freely of all things, you will assist so largely in protecting yourself.

When I learned that it was to be My privilege to bring about this magnificent Activity of Light, I gave great praise and thanks that the privilege was mine. To think now that mankind has this Glorious Knowledge wherein it not only can learn the Laws of Life, but is given something so beautiful and magnificent to fasten its attention upon that it never again needs to enter into the old way of doing things.

O My precious ones, will you not feel with Me the Glory of the Arisen state and learn to put your attention upon your own ascension for a few minutes every day, and make your calls that you may one day become an

Arisen Being. That does not mean that you will avoid any of the service you are to render, but it does mean that you will have a magnificent goal to attain which will help you so many times in rising up over the so-called problems that you have to face. *Learn to control your attention!*

Would it not be magnificent if every time two people began to quarrel, both of them stopped and turned their attention to their own ascension, seeing the other also as an Arisen Master? O my goodness! Dear ones, if blessed people would do that it would clear the way, it would harmonize mankind so greatly; there would not have to be any wars or any struggles if man would just do that. O dear, they don't seem to be doing it, do they?

How marvelous to know always the I AM Presence is the instantaneous solution to all things. Notice, I have said the *instantaneous* solution. In the I AM Presence all things become one. There is no time or space, and when you make the call for any perfect condition to come forth, know that it is done. Do not question any longer, just accept, and go onward, giving praise and thanks that the I AM Presence is the Great Loving Principle, the Great Ruling Power of all Life. Is it not glorious? Is it not wonderful? Is it not marvelous?

Dear ones, I have felt very powerfully that here is a point of the Law which some of you have forgotten which should be brought to your attention. You are not selfish just because you command and demand perfection for yourself. Remember, when asking for Perfection from the I AM Presence, Perfection of itself is a quality in which no human consciousness can act. Therefore, if you call for perfection for yourself and receive it, which naturally you do after making the call, there can be no selfishness in that Perfection.

And another thing, dear ones, do not become discouraged and give up when the going gets rough. And do not have that sinking feeling in the solar plexus! Just hold yourself absolutely firm and strong against that at all times, because what happens when you permit that to take place is very destructive and negative. When you actually give up you give up the stored up energy in your feeling world, which is just poured forth unqualified in any way, except with the feeling of more or less depression. And then, dear ones, where do you look for energy? You see you do not have any more and as you sometimes say, well, all the life just goes out of everything. Well it does, so why do it, dear ones, when you do not have to pour it forth in that way. It is not the least bit necessary and you can instantly call the Presence into action and have Its Perfection released into your world with the speed of Light.

O dear hearts, I know sometimes from the human standpoint it does seem rather like a long row to hoe, but you just keep after it and you'll hoe it. If you wait for the weeds to grow then you have a tougher time hoeing, so whenever you see a long row ahead of you just sail right in! Blessed ones, certainly if I did it you can also, and all you have to do is call your Presence into action and stand at-one with Its Mighty Light as it floods forth to fill your world, never misqualifying that mighty Power, Radiance and Energy. Then what a world of Joy and Happiness will be yours. No matter what seems to face you, just say: "O just run along, you have no power, just run along." You know, dear ones, when you take that stand you are positively terrifying to destructive things, they just turn white with the Power of Light.

You will observe in that which you do that the ones who love Me most are the ones who follow closest the teachings that I brought. Remember that. The ones who follow Me least many times are the ones who profess to love Me most but care little about the teaching I brought. But this above everything else—regardless of what force you may see acting in an individual, make yourself so masterful that you raise that individual out of any force or any activity that may be less than perfection. If you have no personal desires of your own you will find it very

easy to do that. When your desire is sincere in helping
another, the way is open.

*   *   *

May the everlasting Glory of the Limitless Shadowless
Light pour down and enfold you all. May the Richness,
the Joy, the Purity of the Arisen State become each one's
living Consciousness that each one may go forth now a
free being, holding firmly the Mighty Torch of Light to
light the world into the New Golden Age. My Blessings
always.

XVIII

BE A MONUMENT TO HARMONY
by the Great Divine Director.

In the many ages that We have assisted the mankind of Earth, We have found the greatest difficulty of all in giving the Law without having the personality enter in. Always in the minds of man the lawgiver becomes the personification of the Law given and thus the ideal falls before the idol of human creation. There is only one ideal and that is the Living Presence of God, the I AM within and above you. The idol can be anything other than that which you turn your attention to.

Blessed ones, as long as you look to a human being to pull you out of difficulty you will fall into greater and greater difficulty. Never look to personalities, but only to your I AM Presence. If you look to human personality it is true you may receive temporary assistance, but just as soon as one problem is solved another will take its place and you will go on and onward on the wheel of birth and rebirth, the cosmic wheel of evolution which spins unceasingly, slowly, painfully, bringing about, through long ages, perfect balance.

The best cheer I can bring you is that which will cut you free. Why do you look for medicine to heal your bodies when all that has ever been the matter with any of

161

you has been something that has come forth from the inner through misqualified energy which . you have accepted? Then if that is the case, and I say it is, why will you not call to that Presence of Life which sets aside all time and space and acknowledge nothing but the one Great Omnipotent God-self in each? O precious students, know this: That the beauty and perfection which you so long for is very near at hand, and because of the stand that you have taken mankind shall go forward into the Golden Age without passing from this planet. For many long months that was very gravely doubted by Myself as well as others, for it seemed to us that with conditions upon this planet speeding up and reaching ever more frightful climaxes, it would be impossible for enough harmony to be maintained to hold the balance on the constructive side, but that balance has been maintained, and though you are few in number, you have learned, at least in small measure, to govern yourselves. But I assure you, you have much yet to learn. All the control of your feelings that you have learned is as nothing to the control that must be gained, for remember, blessed ones, there is nothing that you can aspire to less than Perfection if you would follow Us.

May I warn you, whatever story comes to you, whether it comes through some friend, acquaintance, or stranger, give it no power unless it agrees with your plan of perfection. If it does, accept it and amplify it, but when the story is discordant or inharmonious, silence it instantly! By that I do not mean to speak unkindly to the one who brings the story. You do not have to be unkind to them, for it is the force being released through them. You have every right and authority to turn to that force and command it to be still. Do not feel that because you have that privilege you can tell some individual to shut up. That is neither good manners nor Divine Law, but you can tell the force to be silent—and in that connection may I ask that you call to Me.

Now My precious ones, I wish to tell you with all the

Power of My Heart that these magnificent Discourses and Dictations which have been given to you are all *real* and you will do well to study them and apply the Laws given. Do you quite realize what it means when one of the Arisen Beings lowers himself sufficiently into the physical octave to flash Letters of Light? Do you quite realize what that means? I think not. Examine your feelings and call the I AM Presence as never before to charge you with such Peace and Harmony that you will go forth with all your energy harnessed and put to perfect use.

Children of Light, My blessed children, the new day has come, and although only a handful recognize that Perfection which is dawning, how great is their privilege in being the first ones. If you could see with Our eyes for just a few minutes you would rejoice with tears in your eyes. There is nothing that you could lack that one call would not bring to you if you would remain harmonious. There is nothing more important than the maintaining of harmony in your worlds, for harmony is the monument on which you all work as one. You can never let your feelings pour one way, your attention another, and your physical body go still another, for then you are a house divided against itself; but if you will follow instead the Law of Harmony, you obey the Law of the One, to pour forth Love, to be at Peace, to look forward and ever upward, that you may not only go forward yourself but be an inspiration for others who know you.

Children of the Light, Rejoice! Lift up your heads and sing a great song, a song of adoration and thanksgiving, of eternal gratitude. Let not your minds be disturbed with questions as to what this, and why would such and such have to occur. Put those questions from your mind and rejoice. Let your feelings be free. Let yourself feel the great Light now pouring forth to bathe your world and flood you with liquid Fire which will set you in such a perfect activity that you will never again have to feel a sense of separation from your Great Presence.

Blessed ones, obey these Laws which have been given to you and which shall be given to you hereafter. Obey no human being unless that one represents these Laws to you, and then only so far as the one representing the Law obeys the Law given. Do not make yourselves slaves to human beings. You do not have to. Stand guard over your feelings and work in harmonizing yourselves. Be prepared to lead, to be calm in blazing forth the Light, in being the fulfillment of the Law.

I plead with you, My children, put aside thoughts of self; what matter where someone stands, of what matter what someone says. There is only one thing that matters and that is more Light, greater and greater Light poured forth. Think well upon that. Do not for a minute, dear ones, think that We, because We do not use a destructive force, have no power to act in a cosmic emergency for this planet. In many countries We have acted and always We use the energy supplied Us by human beings. Watch and see. Behold the action in various countries. You will see very shortly great floods, earthquakes, fires, and storms. You will see the forces of the elements unleashed upon portions of mankind that refuse to obey God's Law. Famine and hunger will appear before you and all manner of appearances that have no power to you who know this Law. Stand with all the love that you have. You shall see how those who deny God's Law will find that that Law is never mocked. God's name is never taken in vain. I AM is that Law, and he who misuses that Mighty Name shall pay in full!

Precious ones, always be kind, and as you gain momentum in power, remember even more carefully to be kind. So many times, I have seen it Myself on hundreds and thousands of occasions, as We train a student here and there to maintain greater harmony, to release greater and greater Love and Light, the student, gaining a momentum in that direction, often becomes aloof from his fellow beings; and feeling that power surging through him, would forget that his fellow beings were as he. Never do that, precious ones. Remember, the I AM Presence raises up, it is the human that takes you down. Love the Light. Love the Arisen Masters, if you will raise yourself, but forget that love, forget the kindness and humility that must be poured forth and you will sink lower and lower, for you will fall rapidly until you reach the lowest depths.

Precious ones, release the full power of your energies now and call that you may have sufficient energy to last you through the day, to carry you onward in all that must be done. Should you ever feel a sudden lack of energy, call to your Presence and to the Great Maha Chohan, Who has promised you to give assistance in that respect. Call to Saint Germain to guide your footsteps, and call to Me, precious ones, if you ever feel that there is a force acting which you wish to silence. I can help you. If you think that My Power is not real, if you think that these Words which are being given are human in their origin, then blessed ones I cannot help you. But if you are willing to stand together as one and apply these laws, you can singly and as a group render the greatest service that can be imagined.

Now that these laws are being simplified for your understanding, now that you can comprehend how We can be real and at the same time not physical, but tangible, and tangible enough for you to touch and see, blessed ones, do you comprehend the glory that sets before you? One day as you are harmonious enough, now that you are learning to focus your attention upon the Inner rather than the outer, you will see Me just as tangibly, just as perfectly as you see one another, for it will be possible, when you are harmonious enough, for the vibratory action to be raised in the optic nerve of each one which will bring Us before you. Do you think that because I say that I have a secret feeling that you cannot become harmonious enough, and therefore that is being said only to lead you on? Beware blessed ones, against those subtle human suggestions that drive in. Stand guard and throw out doubt and fear. They are really one activity, for one cannot act without the other being present. I know full well the forces that act upon the children of Earth. I have watched them for centuries. I know how easy it is for the attention to be turned to the appearance world and for the appearance world, therefore, to take full sway; but I know too how easy it is, with the Power of the I AM Presence released through you, to recognize that oneness and rise out of the discord. This same process every Arisen Master has come through and you are in that same process. How magnificent! How glorious that the way is open, that every step that you have taken will never have to be retaken, that you are going forward in such Joyous company to your own eternal Victory!

Do you think that I am not real? Turn your attention to these words. Study them. Think well upon them. Apply them, and you will see the great glory that is before you. There is nothing unreal about this instruction, precious ones. I have watched doubt and fear hold sway over mankind until now mankind is so enmeshed in that tremendous discordant feeling that the only way it can rise out of it is by belligerent action—it thinks. Then bestir yourselves, precious ones, and remain at Harmony and at Peace with each other, with yourselves. Apply! Call to the I AM Presence!

You have to make your own effort, dear ones. You have to apply these laws by yourself, no one can apply them for you. Then rejoice, for your rejoicing itself is part of the Law, and recognize that oneness, the oneness between yourself and your own Divinity, the Magic Presence; the oneness between yourself and every other human being; the oneness between yourself and the Great Cosmic Space where you are all one. Accept that, feel that oneness, and then claim your God Authority, command God Perfection for yourself and for every part of you.

Now precious ones, just one word of caution. I have stressed that you should call to your Presence. Do not become fanatical, I plead with you. I have watched precious ones who are first fanatical in one way—they do not believe there is a God, therefore why call? Then fanatical in another way—God is there, therefore, they are calling for everything under the sun, and become off balance in that direction—because they do not seek to discipline themselves but rather they wish to be excited in their feelings. Calm your feelings! Stifle those emotions which pour forth from you so quickly at the slightest provocation. Harness them, and then pour forth nothing but Love, and then when you call your I AM Presence you will have instantaneous results. Everything you require, everything you desire can be brought to you so swiftly. Take your attention off the appearances and accept the Fullness of Light within yourself.

I wish you to feel and accept the Love from My Heart flowing forth to envelop you in its Mantle of Protection which will guard you against any human thing if you will let it. Feel yourself charged with My Own energy, with the very Substance of Golden Light from My Electronic Body. Feel yourself at-one with Me, for I AM the Great Divine Director to you as to all men. I AM *within* you as is your Presence. I AM *above* you as is your Presence. I AM at the same level as your Presence and represent the Great Divine Director to you as to all mankind.

XIX

OPPORTUNITY KNOCKS
CONSTANTLY AT YOUR DOOR

by Nada

How beautiful, how magnificent it is to know that now that you have turned the attention to the I AM Presence your progress can be without any limit whatsoever, and as you continue to make your own individual application and go forward releasing your own energy, you are upon the certain pathway from which there is no turning back or no turning aside. Is it not beautiful to know that every particle of energy which you release, directed in love to your own God Presence, the I AM, forms a permanent record for your blessing, and when that record becomes powerful enough you will find yourself raised, becoming transfigured, and then move on into the glorious arisen state.

Why are there those who continue to doubt this reality? O why so often do We hear the cry: "If the Arisen Masters are real why do they not come forth and speak to us in their tangible bodies?" Is that not foolish? Many times We do just that, and man does not recognize us, and when We come forth in this fashion through a channel which has been prepared, then man so often questions that such a thing is possible. The obedience to our suggestions will quickly prove the truth of what We say, but the activity of doubt is so strong in man that actually many times it is almost impossible for the Light, even the powerful Light which We wield, to penetrate the wall of resistance which the human has built up throughout the centuries.

There is one thing I would like to bring to your attention tonight which is one of the feeder qualities of the activity of doubt. You are going to be quite surprised, but I am going to tell you that one of the greatest contributing factors to doubt is laziness. The average person who doubts this reality or who doubts his or her own ability to perform a certain given task, is usually too lazy to try it out. So many times you have heard the statement, "Opportunity knocks but once." I tell you that opportunity is beating a constant tattoo upon your door which never stops. All you have to do is apply yourself to your utmost. Never in the history of the world has there been such opportunity for service!

Together with Saint Germain I have worked on many occasions to bring about the activities of cosmic progress. Under the radiation of the Great Divine Director and the Mighty Maha Chohan, with the assistance of Morya El and Kuthumi, We have built many civilizations. I have not always served in My Arisen body and neither has Saint Germain, yet for thousands of years have We worked together, just as some of you have worked together for thousands of years.

When you rise from that limited state in which you now find yourself, you will able to look back down your own lifestream without any limit whatsoever, and then you will see no lapse of time for you will remember every experience you have ever had, if you care to do so. Of course, there will be many experiences in everyone's past that he will not care to dwell upon too much, in fact, there may be some which you will just prefer not to dwell upon at all; but nevertheless, your entire lives of experience will become one and you will see the great

motivating principle in your lifestream which determines
your place of service in the arisen state.

Do you think it is just chance that Saint Germain is
Lord of the Seventh Ray? There have been many who
have questioned that Saint Germain could be Lord of the
Seventh Ray, realizing that He has been Arisen a
comparatively short time, whereas the Seventh Ray has
been in action a much longer time. Think well upon that
and you will find a magnificent Truth and a magnificent
opportunity for yourself.

Why is it that with so many when they begin turning
their attention and their love in service to the I AM
Presence that they become haughty and arrogant and feel
that no one else has the same privilege? Is it not strange?
To really pour forth love to the I AM Presence is the
greatest privilege of everyone, but how can that make a
person arrogant? For if love is really given it should make
one humble and extremely grateful. Then also, does it
not seem strange that since that information has been
given, so many who understand that portion of it have
chosen to believe that there can be no other service
besides that? How little understanding of life is contained
in the mind of one who refuses to give a blessing to a
brother or sister in the Light. Does he not see that to
pour forth love and blessing to another is in one measure
pouring forth love and gratitude to God, the Great I AM
Presence, which is one with all?

Dear ones, this day (Mother's Day), means a good
deal more to your planet; for the pure mother love, that
is the love of the mother for the child, and even more
powerful, the love of the child for the mother, has been
up to the present time one of the most powerful
purifying activities of which this planet has had the
benefit. O what a great blessing when man will come to
realize the true beauty and perfection in the activity of
motherhood; when the blessed mothers throughout the
planet will accept the great privilege they have in bringing
forth the new forms which are to carry the child of God,

and when the children of God accept their own Divinity and the Divinity of their own blessed mothers, then what a joyous activity will be upon this planet you may be certain.

One of the unfortunate things that has crept in is the subtle feeling of possession which the mother has for her children, which is, of course, the invitation to the sinister force to break that possession. What a marvelous thing when the mother learns never to possess but always to *give*, for that is the way to bring mother and child together in love and gratitude.

Dear ones, most of you have been mothers and fathers at one time or another, and I think without exception each one has had the experience. Will you then on this day of all days feel the tremendous privilege that is yours in getting the Peace of mother love through from your Presence that it may flow forth from you in a mighty river of force to raise the consciousness of mankind everywhere? When you accept that all who are in embodiment are your children and that you stand as a great Cosmic Mother, then you will have the attitude which is correct not only for all mankind but for your own children, for dear ones, I assure you that in the cosmic attitude of Love the mother is the child and the child is the mother. There is no possession but only a great Infinite Love which Blesses, Vivifies, and Purifies forever. If you can accept all that the word "Mother" means and with your heart in tune with that meaning pour it forth, you will render one of the greatest services to man that could well be given.

My deepest Love and Blessings enfold you. Know that God in you is your absolute certain Victory. Know that the Presence of God as represented by the Arisen Masters is your absolute Victory sustained. My Love enfolds you now and always. I thank you.

XX

INNOCENCE—A PROTECTION
by the Goddess of Innocence.

From the Heart of the Great Central Sun I greet you on Rays of Cosmic Love and bless you infinitely for the stand you have made for the Light. Dear people of Earth, know always that Purity is possible. Know that purity is strength, and know that the quality of Innocence, which is the quality I represent to this planet, is one which becomes you from childhood to what you term old age. Do not be afraid of innocence. Innocence lies inside your heart when your motive is pure. If you will call to Me when you are disturbed or confused about the motive that you appear to have at any given point, that Innocence which you require will help to clarify the motive which perhaps you may not understand at the moment.

The time has come in the cosmic life of your planet when those individuals of innocent motive will be protected automatically by the Great Cosmic Law. Those individuals whose motives are selfish and inharmonious, whose motives are destructive, will find that they have no protection against their own ultimate destruction. Do not be afraid of being innocent. It is not necessary, dear ones, that you comprehend all activities. Comprehension, understanding, is only a small part of the Law of Living. If your motive is correct the Law of Life will see to it that you are protected, and although your understanding may not be complete, your life will be, for you will go forward protected, operating with divine wisdom, even though the details of understanding be missing.

Never desire to be too clever. Be kind and loving, as your friend, Saint Germain, has so often prompted you. Be innocent in your desires with one another. Love each other from the heart, and bless each other in your calls for Light and Love. Let that blessing flow out to help mankind, which is in most direful need of greater love and greater innocence. Be pure in your bodies, but most particularly be pure in your minds. Let your motives come from your heart and you will always have the courage to move forward through any appearance of discord. If you will call to Me and accept the radiation of Innocence which I bring, you will find a simplicity of life coming to you that will bring the solution to your problems even before you know the problem exists.

You will find great Friends rising up to help you, Who will protect you and guard you often from dangers you do not know exist, because in your innocence and in your purity the Light itself comes to your defense. The Light which fills the hearts and minds of individuals, although they may not be on the conscious pathway, will be the Light which will guide them and sustain them and protect them as they move onward to their Victory.

Do not hesitate to call on Me, for I am thrilled to be of service to you. It has been a long time since I have had the privilege of working with a group at the physical level. Human beings on this planet have been most desirous of not being innocent, but the desires of your hearts, which are more powerful than the thoughts of your heads, have made possible My coming to you in this fashion, and you may call on Me as frequently as you wish, for I am with you and will help you in what you are to do.

Dear ones, know the beauty and perfection of being Innocent, and accept My Love and Blessings now and always.

XXI

PURITY–A NATURAL STATE

by the Goddess of Purity

It has been a very long time since it was possible for Me to come very far into the atmosphere of Earth, and certainly it has been a long time since it was possible for any but those who work most closely with the children of Earth to penetrate into the thickness and the blackness of this particular area. How great is My Joy at being with you tonight you cannot know, yet how wonderful it is to see even the few who are here cleanse themselves sufficiently to make it possible for Me to come and be at-one with you.

Dear ones, how We long for the day when all humanity will know the joy of being Pure, physically, mentally, emotionally, and spiritually. O, We know it is not an easy thing, but We also know that in the calls, in the earnest determination of the sincere student to his own I AM Presence and to the Arisen Host, all things are possible. Beloved ones, as you turn your attention to the I AM Presence each day and become increasingly aware of that scintillating reality, likewise become increasingly aware of the Presence of the Arisen Masters who are working with you. You should become as aware of Us, though you may not see Us with your physical sight, as

174

you are of the sunlight, and the rain, and the soft presence of the winds that blow.

Beloved ones, you may be certain that the natural state of humanity is to be Pure, and in that Purity, when it is correctly understood, lies the greatest happiness of all. What a great mistake humanity has made through so many centuries, believing that it had to maintain a very close contact with dirt and filth in order to be natural. O blessed ones, the natural thing for humanity is to be God-like, to be Pure and at-one with the Eternal Light of God that never fails!

Purity does not consist entirely of rigorous control over one's self. It also consists of a simple outpouring of love to the Godhead, to the Masters, and to your fellow-men. In the Purity of unselfish Love is the reality of perfection, and your progress will be much more swift and much more certain when you understand those simple words.

How gratified I am to be among you tonight and to see in the radiation which you pour forth the progress you have made. O dear ones, of course in the physical rate of vibratory action where you dwell and where your consciousness is maintained at the present time, there are certain densities of vibration that often make you feel that you are far from Pure, and there are many temptations, mostly, believe Me, through carelessness, that cause you often to feel that you have not done all that you might. Yet, dear ones, I assure you that in the simplicity of turning to your own Radiant God-self, to your own I AM Presence, is the Purity, the strength, the power, and the Light that will take you forward swiftly and surely into every victory. Call to Me and I will help you.

The day will come, blessed ones, when dust and dirt as you know it today will cease to exist upon this planet. The atmosphere will be clear and pure and sparkling with Light, and humanity, of course, will feel and experience the joy of the freedom that will bring.

Dear ones, a word of caution: It is very easy for anyone in physical embodiment to look upon the activity of another and pass judgment upon that activity saying, "Well, this one has that responsibility and this other one should be doing this, and why are they not doing it?" Dear ones, you do not know from your limited human standpoint whether or not the individual upon whom you are passing judgment is performing his or her duties; therefore, do not pass judgment, but give of your love to that individual, especially to that one who seems to need your assistance. Do not be afraid, beloved ones, of loving one another. Do not be afraid of turning to that Great Presence which beats your heart and calling to it for the fullness of Love, Light, Peace, and Purity. Accept it in your world today. Believe Me, O My beloved children, this is not something strange which will cause you to be different from the rest of humanity according to their outward appearance, their outward way of looking at you. No, dear ones. If you but obey the Laws which Saint Germain has given to you and follow the suggestions others of Us have placed in your keeping from time to time, you will rise into the highest type of human beings, and be at-one with the Great Creative Principle; through your purification and the increase in your vibratory action you will swiftly and surely rise into your ultimate Perfection.

Beloved ones, you may be certain that as the minds and hearts of humanity are purified, the physical filth which often accompanies humanity will disappear. Those things which your attention is upon will be brought forth, and if you sincerely in your heart desire Perfection, Light, Beauty, Purity, Love, those things will be given to you. Remember, you cannot receive that which you are not willing to give away. In the purity of your desire make certain that your desire is equally powerful for others that they too may climb. Desire for self-advancement is not pure unless the gratitude is to the Presence and the Masters first, and the hand is held out to your fellow travelers on the pathway. Do not think that when I say "fellow travelers" I am referring in any way to the activity of certain individuals who have been misled by the cunning propaganda of those who seek to enslave humanity and to inflict their hold upon the human mind. I speak of those who are your brothers in the Light and who are fellow travelers with you into the Realms of Beauty and Perfection.

The conditions which humanity faces, especially in eastern and southern Europe, and in western Asia, are appalling. You in the beauty and the comparative tranquility of your surroundings cannot begin to appreciate the vast difference that exists between the situation as you face it today and the situation being faced by thousands upon thousands upon thousands of your fellow men. Conditions have never been more dreadful on this planet, but you may be certain that it is always darkest just before the dawn. You may be certain, or I would not be with you tonight, that already the first faint glimmerings of a New Golden Age are tinting the eastern horizon of the progress of the world. Hope is not yet dead in the hearts of humanity. They are grasping at straws today, but Hope is still alive within their hearts. How they need, oh dear ones, how they need the example of individuals who have learned sufficient mastery to travel in Purity and in Peace, in Understanding and in Tolerance among them.

O dear ones, even though you see it imperfectly from your standpoint, even though you comprehend but partially from your human situation, believe Me when I tell you that this Light is very real and We are with you in your progress as you go forward step by step. One day you will know how real We are!

Blessed ones, stand with that ever Blazing Light! Feel it! Acknowledge it at all times, and as I said to you earlier this evening, become aware of Our nearness to you. Be conscious of the fact that We are working closely and at-one with you, and then there will grow up within you the courage, the strength, the unalterable Peace that comes with *knowing* that you *know*. Never forget that even though We are Arisen and from the standpoint of humanity above error, still We are not above the I AM Presence; and even as you turn to that Great Presence of Light within you so do We acknowledge our oneness with that Light, and call to that I AM that I AM that We may give ever more of Ourselves in Love, in Understanding, in Happiness, and in Peace. My Love enfolds you.

XXII

FREEDOM
by Saint Germain.

I bring you greetings from the Great Chohans of the Rays, the Gods of the Mountains, the Gods of the Elements, from the many who are assembling at the Royal Teton, and from many more who are yet to come. I bring you a special greeting from the Great Maha Chohan and from these Mighty Friends of yours.

Man's experience upon this Earth has been for many centuries a constant reproof to each individual, for the experiences of the outer world have constantly led to greater and greater disturbance, to greater war and destruction. Century after century has mankind upon this Earth turned its attention upon the acquiring of wealth, the acquiring of power, the acquiring of one thing or another. Century after century has man turned his attention upon self, recognizing ever so slightly his own God power, but claiming falsely and humanly God's power in order that selfish ends might be attained.

Out of the great seething mass of humanity which has peopled this Earth since its beginning there has arisen one group, and this group in part is responsible to a large degree for the progress that has been made upon this planet. This group is very large and it represents those who have always stood for the Light. Outside of this group have always been many more who do not give heed

179

to those finer but more powerful feelings of love within them, and have ever sought upon the outer pathway to acquire happiness and peace. Many thousands of years ago I determined to bring forth some place, some time upon this planet a great Nation of Arisen Masters, and with that purpose before Me I went through many trying experiences striving ever to illumine those who were near Me, striving ever "To Know, to Dare, to Do, and to be Silent."

Now it seems to Me in spite of all the disturbance, in spite of all the disorder, the lack of cooperation, in spite of all these things, still I shall establish a great Nation of Arisen Masters, and the time is ripe for that to come forth right now. Watch and see!

At the turn of the century, We in the Arisen state, those of Us who have had to deal mostly with mankind in their comings and goings upon this world, observing the great Cosmic Law in action and seeing that the days of this planet were numbered unless Peace could come for the planet, determined upon releasing the fullness of Our Understanding to the humanity of Earth, which same Understanding released would enable those whose Light was great enough to grasp the Scepter of Dominion and be free. Due to the position which I maintained as a humble Messenger of God upon the Seventh Ray to this Earth, it fell to My lot to be the Directing Master for the incoming Golden Age. This Golden Age I am to direct from the Arisen state, even though there may be many assisting who are yet unarisen.

Looking about for those strong enough to carry this great Light to release it to humanity, I came upon My children of long ago, your Beloved Messengers, and so I watched them and worked with them, always from the Inner realms, for never were they consciously aware of My assistance to them; and had you known them at that time you would have observed that consciously they were not aware of My assistance.

In order that they might be Messengers of Mine it was

necessary that they learn to renounce the world and all things that the world had to offer them, and thus they went through experiences in one short embodiment which would have filled many embodiments had I not been assisting them. Many times they were in one position, many times in another, but always were they learning. I directed their footsteps from shore to shore and led them always. It soon became apparent that My beloved son, whom you know as Godfre Ray King, would prove to be the one through whom this great Truth should be released. When that became apparent I reported My findings to My Master, the Great Divine Director, and He, looking upon the scene said: "I do not believe it can be done." "Nevertheless," I said, "I shall try it out," and then He said: "Very well, separate Godfre from the outer world, from all outer things, and let us observe what happens." Thus it became necessary for Godfre to leave his home, and although he did not know why, he found himself in California, and there the real unfoldment began.

Through a Blessed one whose name I may not disclose, inspiration was given to your former Messenger, Arisen now, which led him to the foot of Shasta, and there the experiences recorded in *Unveiled Mysteries* took place. You must remember always that those experiences are from the Realm of Light, that they are not human experiences but rather Divine experiences in which a human consciousness played a part.

Then, with many other magnificent Laws released, I brought Godfre and Lotus together again. I do not wish to convey to you the intimate story of their private lives, but this I do wish you to know. They, together, formed the most powerful Focus that had ever been established upon this planet since the time of your Blessed Master Jesus; and the two of them together, although an occasional error crept in, still the errors, few in number, can be overlooked, largely because of the great good which was accomplished.

It is true that many who did not apply the Law as I gave it forth through them found occasion to criticize, to condemn, to pass judgment, and many and many a time would I hear the cry go up: "I do not think that an Arisen Master could have said such a thing." As I have said, perhaps a few errors did creep in, but whatever they may have been they were small compared to the great power released. You might say to Me. "How could errors creep in if it was an Arisen Master activity?" and I say to you, as I have said before: Until one reaches the Arisen state, regardless of who they are, regardless of the position they maintain, still are they subject to making mistakes. If they accept the mistakes then they will be no bigger than their mistakes, but if they refuse acceptance of them, call on the Law of Forgiveness, rise above them and go on, mankind will remember them, not for their mistakes but for their Victories!

After training My Messengers from the inner standpoint for thirty years, I came forth to them tangibly and worked with them, establishing a mighty Focus of Light through them. I gave them five years to perform My task. At the end of that time they were to retire, but when that time arrived they refused to do so, knowing the great need of the world and feeling that if they stayed in active service they could render a greater service than before. They asked My permission and, of course, since it is never My power to command but only to govern in Love, I explained what would take place in either case, should they go on in their outer service or should they retire from the outer world. Having heard Me through, they decided to go on and I promised to continue to assist them when I could.

*   *   *

I can say this to you at this time—bear it well in your consciousness. Every nation, every government upon this planet that does not serve the Light, that will not recognize a power greater than itself, that refuses to give Liberty and Love to its people, shall perish! Every one! Those which are most powerful will destroy those which are least powerful, and then the ones that are most powerful will destroy one another, until finally humanity upon this Earth will learn, as they once knew thousands of years ago, that *God alone is Great*, that the Light is Eternal, and that Love is real.

Every second of this embodiment from now on can be spent in transcendent service to mankind. You do not have to preach. You do not have to stand forth to perform a miracle. All you have to do is *live* this Law, and live it so beautifully that you cause others to do likewise. You are My children. For every unselfish, beautiful thing that you do I pour forth My Love in an unending stream to you, but when you persist in wasting your energy in turning your attention upon things of little moment, when you persist in arguing, when you persist in seeing the false in one another, I cannot help you, for I help the one most who feels himself nearest to Me, who Loves Me greatest and wants My assistance sufficiently to recognize My qualities in himself.

Whether or not you know I am real, still do you know that these Words are real. Then give heed and learn now to silence your human self. Learn to pour forth a constant stream of Love to all things. Learn to live in Harmony and Peace with one another. Then as you do that you will find yourself coming together building a New City, expanding it without any limit whatsoever, and all those who come within your radiant embrace will accept the Light through your Love, and stand with you to bring in the New Golden Age.

When you learn, beloved ones, to open your heart, and there centering your consciousness behold the Universe, when you learn that and then know, "I AM the Oneness of all things," you will have found the Open Doorway into the realm of Freedom.

O precious ones, no longer look to the outer world;

no longer seek for God or His Messengers, the Arisen Masters, in the outer world, but look within yourself. Accept the full Power of God within yourself. Accept My Love, My Reality, within yourself and then, and then only will you see that this is not a myth, a dream, or a fantasy. Why, O why cannot blessed ones see that I am real? When beloved ones follow My promptings they have results, yet they cannot quite put their hand upon Me and so they think I am not real. But that is because they accept separation, they constantly accept that there is a vast space between themselves and God. I tell you there is no space, there is no time, all things are one. If you will turn within yourself and there, sitting within the silence of your room, expand that Inner world, expand it and expand it until you see within yourself the entire Universe and all that is, not as something tiny, but as something vast—for I assure you the Inner World is very vast—then in your stillness, in your great Love, will all things become clear to you and you will see Our Great Reality. You cannot understand it in your mind alone, but you can see it in your feelings, and you can know it with your limitless consciousness, your God-conscious-ness within yourself.

*   *   *

The Laws which are given herein are the Eternal Laws of Life, and that shall stand regardless of human beings, regardless of human consciousness, regardless of any change which comes one way or another. These Laws shall stand, and those who follow these Laws shall live a more abundant life and go forward to their Victory.

For each human being upon this planet there will open the way of how he shall go. There are some who will go one way and some another, and those who choose the wrong way will ever have the opportunity to choose again. No individuals are condemned to everlasting torment. There is no hell other than that which you create for yourself. It is not a part of Our activity to pass judgment upon individuals and lead them off into a compound where they shall abide until the end of time. We have no cause for revenge. We have no desire to prove Our power to the rest of mankind that wants so much to know Our reality. We have only one desire, and that is to bless, to heal, to strengthen, and to encourage. We have only the desire of *being* the Light.

There is nothing more glorious than the Light. There is nothing more real than your determination to hold to the highest ideals of the Arisen Masters. Those are the ideals more precious to you than gold or jewels. Those ideals are the Great Reality of Life. Do not hesitate to take your stand with all the love and determination of your being that those ideals of Love, Beauty, and Perfection shall abide within you forever.

*   *   *

Out of the Realm of Light cometh all things, and into the Light all things eventually return. Having expressed more Light, all things become One, and thus you must claim yourself as a part of the Great Central Sun. O Thou Great Enfolding Light, raise the consciousness of each. Let them know that, see that, understand that, O Wonrous I AM.

Feel your heart as the Great Central Sun and see its Myriad Rays weaving a Celestial Blanket of Light to enfold your planet. See yourself as a Cosmic Being. Accept your Divine responsibility. Accept your own instantaneous activity. Accept your own reality in Us.

Before Thy Ever Present All-expanding Light, O Great I AM, we bow, accepting Thee in all things forever. I thank Thee.

XXIII

AN ELOHIM COMES TO EARTH'S AID
by Arcturus.

I have been traveling freely in the atmosphere of your planet for some days examining the situation which exists here. You have been told by Saint Germain that conditions are far better than you believe outwardly, and that is indeed the case. Nonetheless, even though progress has been made, the conditions which exist in your world arising from human ignorance and human failings are conditions profoundly to be regretted and earnestly to be corrected.

In traveling about your planet I have observed much cause for discord, misunderstanding between nations, between races, between religions and creeds, between military cliques in fact, dear ones, this unhappy planet contains cause for discord that arises almost momentarily between almost all individuals. I am, therefore, setting aside certain laws which have governed this planet up to this time, which will make it easier for the humanity here to rise out of some of its appearances of limitation and accept for itself the full Power of God in action, which will ultimately mean its Freedom and Victory.

Dear ones, humanity has accepted here for countless thousands of years a great inequality between male and female. This inequality I am removing at this time. The differences between men and women will cease to exist and the individuals on this planet will come into a pattern of divine order which will make it possible for them to understand each other better. It is even proverbial among you that it is difficult for men to understand women, and it is difficult for women to understand men. This appearance of difficulty has been built up willfully and made much of during countless centuries, and upon it has been built much of the discord in the world. You will see these things coming about for I have uttered an unalterable decree that this be done. You will understand one another and the desire for God's Kingdom, for Heaven on Earth, will permeate the atmosphere of this planet so that human desires and the gratification of the senses will become of less importance. Only thus can men rise into an understanding where they know themselves and in that knowledge rise into their perfect Victory.

The humanity who live here in this "heart land" of the world must awaken to the power which they wield as individuals, and once awake they must let that power flow forth to influence and encourage the remainder of humanity on this planet. Too long have there been doubts and fears here in the United States of America as to what is the right course and what is the wrong course. By these debates between what is right and what is wrong humanity vacillates back and forth and ends up in despair and disgust. America must awaken and go forward powerfully and certainly to its Victory!

In reality the other nations of the world who often times appear to try to stop the course of your country are but in turn trying to pattern themselves after what they believe to be the courses set forth here. The cry of the people of Earth, the despairing wail that has come up from this planet, is being answered by the Great White Brotherhood. Yes, We will come forth, if need be wearing Bright Armor and clad so that all men may know Us, so that this world may rise to its predestined place of

Perfection and this Universe go forth on schedule to the
development of all good and perfect things herein and
hereafter!

Your planet is now taking on the quality that it must
take with respect to the other planets in this solar system.
Even as the differences between male and female here on
this planet were set aside, so are those differences set
aside among the planets of this system. Too long has the
Earth been held by indecision, been torn by conflicting
doubts and fears. It now rises by the Power of Light re-
released both from Our octave and from your octave here.
As students go forward with sincere hearts, the Earth
takes on the quality that is required in the New Age and
finds its rightful place amid the Music of the Spheres.

Blessed people of this Earth, listen to what I tell you.
The intentions of the heart are the important, the
all-enfolding, the all-consuming items which concern an
Arisen Master. Never forget that! As you think and *feel* in
your heart, so will you become. The actions which you
perform are but the playing of shadows upon shifting
sands. There is no permanency in your physical act or
deed. The only permanency, blessed ones, is that which is
within your heart, for you come into this world with
that heart and when you leave you take the heart with
you, for you and your heart are one, even as God and I
AM are one.

Live as beings of Light alone! Live as beings of cause,
letting your Love flow forth! I wish to make this point
emphatically clear: The outflowing of Love is not a soft,
weak, limp activity of life; it is not surrender; it is not an
acceptance of evil; it is not the making of excuses for
failure. The outflowing of Love, dear students, is the proof
that you are winning that Victory here in the
physical octave where all may observe your progress,
where you become not an individual example but a group
example. Dear ones, watch yourselves that you do not
become fanatical in your determination to follow the
Light.

The answer to every problem is in your heart. The solution of every difficulty is in your call to the Presence. The Victory of every attempted task is in the sincerity of your desire.

> Rise up and face Life glowing from within!
> Knowing the fullness of Love's beauty,
> Being the full expression of all life!
> Let your Joy flow out and you become the Conquer-
>   ing Presence!
> Dissolving all discord and appearance
>   and move on and up,
> Awakening mankind by the example which you set.
> Humanity longs for Joy, it longs for Love, it
>   longs for Peace
> And it denies these very things
> Even while it longs for them.
> BE the Law! And let your Light shine!

. . .

Note: Arcturus is one of those Great Cosmic Beings known as an Elohim. The entire humanity of this Earth owes Him a great deal. Many millions of years ago that Great and Mighty One, by His own individual action, made possible this particular planet on which you reside. Had it not been for Him and His own choice in this matter, there are countless thousands inhabiting the Earth today who would not have had the opportunity of gaining their own Victory. The Law of their lives would have been revoked had it not been for His intercession at that far distant date.

Arcturus is the Master in charge of a great solar system, which is beyond that which is known to us as the Star Arcturus. Arcturus is placed in authority over this great solar system, and stands in the same position to that solar system as the Silent Watcher does to this One. He is not a star as such, but radiates His control over that star and the planets around it. There is a relation between this solar system and the solar system which Arcturus represents.

—Saint Germain

XXIV

BRINGING VICTORY HOME
by Victory.

In attaining your Mastery remember always that you must have all qualities of perfection acting within you. You have learned through much experience and some pain the activity of Love. Now learn Wisdom and Power, that the Unfed Flame may come forth tangibly in your midst.

When something stands in your way when you have received a prompting from your Presence or from some of Us, know that the reason it is not forthcoming is some place in your own world. But know too that it is far better to give one decree and mean it—and I mean that! Take your positive, joyous stand. Call your I AM Presence into action for every condition. Learn to manifest Perfection and be the example of this Law. You have used that very human and very earthy expression—"you do not accept hair tonic from a barber who is bald." The same is true in this activity of Light. If you wish others to accept the Light, you must *be* the Light yourself. Remember this too, and you will find it of very valuable assistance: *Do nothing when you are alone that you would not do before the presence of others!* When you go by yourself to give your Love and

191

adoration to your Presence, do it! Do not waste your time when you have God-given moments to release that Light and Love from your Presence in an unending stream to be a blessing to you and to all mankind. Be honest, honorable, and straightforward in all things. Observe silence, and there is nothing that you cannot do.

Accept your responsibility. Realize that when you accept the responsibility for doing a certain thing that you have pledged that God will do that thing. Then it is up to you, as part of God, to see that it is accomplished to the best of God's ability. Remember your oneness with your own I AM Presence and accept no human thing.

Learn to be true to your word even in small things. For instance, if you tell some one that you will meet them at such and such a time, if you make a promise that you will write a letter or some such thing, then do it if the heavens fall. Do it if you have to put aside every other thing you wish to do. Do it! If you pledge yourself to any specific thing, do it! Do not give any promise lightly, but when it is given follow it through, otherwise you will never be dependable, and We cannot use those who are not dependable.

As you have been told by your Beloved Saint Germain, a portion of the old occult law is being reestablished for the children of the Earth. Reestablishing this form will bring a surer, safer way for the advancement of the children of Earth into the glorious arms of their own Presence, and from this time on it will be possible for Me to work in much closer conjunction with those who wish My activity in their worlds.

May I remind you that there is no higher obligation to any individual anywhere upon any of the vast planets which fill the great universe than the obligation, the privilege, and the joy of pouring forth Love to his Creator, the I AM Presence, and then to all created things. Recognizing the Presence as being at-one with all Life is a very simple way of clearing from your worlds

forever the feeling that individuals sometimes have power
to act in your world whether you like it or not; for
recognizing the God Presence and God Principle acting in
each one and giving power only to that, you quickly set
aside any human creation, and only the Light will have its
dominion wherever you move.

Saint Germain has explained to you just what is
meant by the seven degrees of consciousness and I wish
to explain to you just how certain colors and rates of
vibratory action coinside with those degrees of
consciousness so that the matter of color may be cleared
up in your mind once and for all.

You have been told that the activity of black and red
is never an Arisen Master activity, and that is perfectly
true, because it is only as we cross the line from the
human into the Divine, or to bring it to you in words
more near to what Saint Germain has recently given you,
it is only when you cross the line from the third degree
into the fourth degree that you move out of the human
sufficiently to recognize a power greater than human as
having action. From that time on the individual will not
use the colors of red or black unless a specific service is to
be rendered thereby. And you will find that black is not a
color, and many times there are those who think they are
using black who are really using a dark shade of blue,
which is of course, entirely correct.

Now the activity of red aligns itself with the first
degree of consciousness. The activity of blue with the
second degree. The activity of yellow or gold comes
through the third degree, and thus you see the first
primary colors are released in the first primary activity of
the unfolding consciousness in physical embodiment.
Then crossing the line we come next to the activity and
color of pink, which is the beginning of the love element
acting. We go from there to the green at the fifth degree.
The sixth brings us indigo, and the seventh violet. The
activity of white always represents the Great White
Brotherhood, and really there is no pure white anywhere

in the physical octave. Pure white occurs only at the Inner levels, but naturally it is a magnificent thing to approach as near the pure white as it is possible from the standpoint of the human.

I wish you to remember, blessed ones, that your Password into or out of any activity or situation is always the same, regardless of the point of attainment you have reached. This Password is "I AM" and as you understand the fullness of the meaning of those words, you will raise yourself in consciousness until all things are open to you. All points anywhere in the universe may be visited by you freely and at will. All will obey your own behest of Love, and your world will be in Divine Order as you fully comprehend the meaning of those great words, "I AM." In giving you this statement tonight I call upon you particularly to watch yourselves to see to it that you do not at any time use them lightly or promiscuously. Those words carry the most powerful vibratory action of any words in the physical octave and you must remember that they are Sacred Words released into your keeping as a Sacred Trust. Use them, but use them with all reverence and all understanding that you may never misuse or fail to use the Great Law concerning them.

Dear ones, remember too, that while you have learned the Law of Forgiveness, until you have learned to forgive another you yourself cannot be forgiven!

Blessed ones, you little realize the magnificence and Glory of this Tunnel of Light you have been visualizing and calling forth, which reaches from your Center here to the Royal Teton. Well, blessed ones, I think you will rejoice when you know that the activity which you have been tuning into is not only a matter of your visualization but it has become a Reality, and it is a more far-reaching reality than you dream. It is through just such an activity that We who serve principally upon the neighbor planet Venus journey safely across space to render a service here. Although it may seem to you rather strange that these inner things which apparently have no outer reality can be true, yet I tell you they can be and are true, and when you yourself discipline yourself sufficiently you will have the reality of these Truths released into your own consciousness.

Blessed ones, tonight at the Royal Teton has already begun the activity of the Conclave, and I shall tell you that at Saint Germain's and My suggestion, the presiding Master for this evening is none other than your own Beloved Godfre, and you will all have the opportunity of moving into the Royal Teton sometime between now and tomorrow morning, though you may not stay there very long.

O beloved ones, when mankind learns the Law of Love, the Law of Joy, the Law of Beauty, it will accept and stand at-one with Us, but until that time it goes on its way in darkness, feeling that there can be no reality in any but physical things, and thus it deprives itself of the Victory of the age, the Joy and Beauty of the Arisen Masters, the Perfection of Life and the attainment of its own Freedom in the Ascension.

Dear ones, with the activity tonight I wish to explain just a little more so that you may understand the nature of what is transpiring. Never in the history of any planet has this privilege been given which is yours tonight, for dear blessed ones, I wish you to know that at the present time I am leaving the planet Earth again to take up My abode on Venus, and you blessed ones who are coming with Me are to serve as an escort to My Home. You have made sufficient progress to be entrusted with this high honor. Think of that the next time the road seems a little difficult for you. Remember that you have been entrusted to bring Victory home and through that activity you yourself will always have Victory. I thank you.

XXV

QUESTIONS AND ANSWERS

by Saint Germain.

Q. On animal and plant life.

A. The plant life, animal life, and the human life are all life and they all come forth at different levels of consciousness in the physical octave, but there is not a passing of one to another in the physical octave in any way. That is, the plant consciousness remains the plant consciousness; the animal consciousness remains the animal consciousness; and the human consciousness, the God consciousness, remains at that level until the ascension takes place. Each goes back to its source and that completes its evolution.

Animal body is one creation, human is one creation. You haven't any more right to call that the animal be released from its body than for the human. The call should never be made that any life be taken from its body. Pour forth Divine Love and kindness at all times. I do not recommend that you have animals about you because of the lower rate of vibration any more than human beings who have not advanced very far. Do not hold the idea that because you associate too much with one animal you get to be like it.

Animal life was released here at the inner levels just

196

the same as the God life of the human, and the plant life, and it is the work of the human consciousness which bound it into the physical octave from the inner. It is the slowing down of the vibratory action which manifests in the physical which is the work of the human consciousness. There are many beautiful and lovely things slowed down in the physical octave, i.e., flowers and birds, but actually there is no Arisen Master activity that is physical, it is all from the inner. The Arisen Masters work to raise the animal on the inner the same as on the physical. They work with the animal consciousness, the plant consciousness, the God consciousness at various levels, also with the Elementals, the Devas, Prince Oromosis.

Animal forms were *not* originally created by black magicians! Many of the animal forms which were created were the product of the human consciousness and human cunning through the black magicians, and that has gone on right up to the present day, believe it or not, but there have been a great many forms of animal life which have come forth for the blessing of man. Man has now passed through the stage where that is any longer a blessing to him and the animal life will be removed from this planet, but that is a matter for those in charge of that kingdom to handle. Make your call for the perfect thing to be done for every animal, and release your love and your blessings always to them. This does not mean now that you must have pets or just get yourself right down into the vibratory action of the animal, for that is the very thing you are trying to get away from. Remember, the animal kingdom upon this planet is a perfectly natural thing and if you will follow the teaching as you find it in *Unveiled Mysteries* with reference to the love that you can pour forth, even to a destructive animal, you will find that the misconception will be very swiftly cleared from your mind for all time.

Q. On fog.

A. The fog is not an activity of blessing to the land, and

that fog which has been coming into this part of the
United States for many years, as well as into other
sections of the country, is a certain type of accumulation
which was generated thousands of years ago by the
inhabitants of this land. Those inhabitants in embodiment at the present time again find that it is necessary,
in order to balance the Law, in order to square themselves as it were; they have to experience some of that
which they created for others, for the fog which you
observe was originally created by those who did not serve
the Light, with the desire to cause a famine, for the fog
was intended to shut out the light of the sun and make it
impossible for things to grow. Your activity concerning it
should be to pour greater and greater blessings to the
elements, particularly to the sylphs and to the undines.
Call for the balancing of all the Nature activities, and
then if you do not see the immediate results that you
desire, just give a blessing, rejoice that you do know the
Law, and then go on your way. You see, actually in the
worlds of many individuals there arises a fog, just as that
that comes into the Golden Gate. It is always a human
creation and has nothing of the Light within it. Even
though the atoms that compose the fog contain Light,
still the energy about them is misqualified and the
ultimate release of that Light is its return into its original
primal state, the pure Light from the Great Central Sun.

Q. Scepter of Dominion.

A. The Scepter of Dominion is your conscious
acknowledgment and use of your own I AM Presence
within you.

Q. Archangels.

A. There are a great company of Archangels, but the
names of only a few are known to you *Archangel
Michael,* Who is referred to as a Lord of the Sun, and
also, a Lord of the Flame, is the Being of the Deva
Kingdom Who has charge of the incoming individual

upon this planet. It is He who has appeared many times before the blessed mothers. His activity is one of great Purity and Love.

The *Archangel Gabriel* is another great member of the Deva Kingdom, Who assists in leading the blessed ones who have just quit physical embodiment into their proper realm of activity.

Lucifer is not an Archangel but a Lord of the Flame whose activity has been the purifying and the cleansing of the mind. The mistaken idea that Lucifer and the devil are one has brought about great unhappiness. The story of the fall of Satan is a reality but it does not deal with Lucifer. This was another being entirely whose name it is not wise to give, who turned aside from the path, after having at one time gained temendous power in the Light.

The Archangels, Angel Devas, Lords of the Flame, Cherubim, and Seraphim are all members of what we refer to as the Deva Kingdom. They are the servants of mankind for they are obedient to those who command in Love through the power of the I AM. Your love and attention to these Great Beings—and many of them are very powerful in their own right and in turn command great legions—will bring many blessings.

Q. Star Astrea and Prince Astrea.

A. The Star Astrea is a great Being, and the Prince Astrea, Whose activity you have known for some time as that of helping to clear the entities from the physical octave, is a Being Who works under the direction of the Great One, Star Astrea. Many times they are mistaken as the same, but they are in reality two separate Beings—one whose activity is Cosmic, and the other whose activity is here upon the Earth at the present time.

Q. Diana.

A. Diana has been referred to as a Goddess of Fire but directly She is not so, although She has served greatly with those elementals who have had to do with the activity of fire. Diana is the blessed one who attained Her Victory during the civilization of Lemuria, and She has assisted mankind more or less closely since that time.

There is a spot not far from San Francisco which was sacred to Diana quite a number of years ago. Many times She returns to this spot and is still to be seen there on occasion. This spot is on the slopes of Mount Tamalpais.

Q. The Secret Love Star.

A. The Secret Love Star is referred to as such because it is, more correctly speaking, a quality released to this planet by a great Cosmic Being whose activity is so transcendant and so Pure and Perfect that He may not render too great an assistance to the children of this Earth because of their great discord. However, because of the need of His quality, the consciousness of the Secret Love Star makes it possible for Him through the consciousness to release His quality of Divine Love, which descends through the atmosphere of earth like a great rainbow. The Secret Love Star has nothing whatsoever to do with the star of Bethlehem, although at that time, because of the quickening of the minds and the attention of the many turned to the heart, a great outpouring of His Radiance was possible. You may consider the Secret Love Star as a great Being, although in reality your contact with Him is only through the quality which He is able to release at the present time. This is a quality of Divine Love so pure that earthly minds cannot comprehend it.

Q. Joseph Smith and the Angel Moroni.

A. The one you refer to as the Angel Moroni is no less a Being than the Archangel Michael. In the first vision of Joseph Smith he observed his own Higher Mental Body, which is the Guardian Angel of each individual. When the Archangel Michael appeared to this blessed one there was one with Him of very transcendent activity Who was at one time the son of Archangel Michael. He also is an Archangel.

Q. On health and disease.

A. The I AM Presence is always the great fount of Wisdom to which the student should turn, for every individual has the great God Presence which will guide him in these matters. I give you the Law, but the greatest Law of all is to turn to the I AM Presence and call for Its use. In this matter of health, the student should always realize the I AM Presence is the great Healing Presence and should never accept any permanency of illness. However, in maintaining balance, he or she can turn to the Presence to receive the absolute guidance there. It is the same with food. There are some who will find that certain things can be eaten with very marvelous results, and those same things would almost serve as poison for another; but the I AM Presence is the one Who understands and will release the promptings to you. Of course, there are certain substances which you cannot put into the body and have the Arisen Master activity come forth. Always call to your Presence.

In order to be Master, it is sometimes wise to know all things, yet remember that all things are contained in the Presence, and when you find an individual case where you feel that a certain revelation to the individual involved would be of help, call your Presence into action and you will have the necessary prompting as to what to do in the case of various so-called diseases. It is wise sometimes to be able to think in terms of the force that is acting when you observe a discordant, an inharmonious or diseased condition. It is still more wise to rise above the appearance and call the Presence into action that it be consumed.

Now then, sickness and disease as such exist in this world because of only two things: misdirected thought and misdirected feeling. Whether that thought and feeling have been released at this particular moment, or whether it is an accumulation of ages past makes no difference. Misdirected energy is responsible for the illness, disease, unhappiness, dissolution and the downfall of mankind.

Misdirected energy is still energy qualified to work and act in a certain fashion. It is your job as a student of this Light under this radiation to call in the name of your Presence, and for the assistance of the Masters if you think advisable, that the energy so qualified be requalified to perfection. Know unmistakably that doubt and fear are basically the causes for every appearance of disease, inharmony, or discord that can exist.

To be specific: A disease germ is the condensation of a thought form. These thought forms were originally lowered into physical vibratory rates of action by black magicians hundreds and hundreds of years ago, and thus these conditions were released into physical bodies. The form of the disease has a very slight relationship to the thoughts and feelings the individual may have at the moment. You may be very certain that regardless of the disease or appearance of disease, the basic cause of it is within the individual, without exception.

If you could see the hospitals and wards of perfectly well human beings with God's own Power lying latent within them, who have made themselves ill as a result of misdirected thought and feeling, it would appall you. I assure you that the reason the insane assylums, hospitals, and institutions for the sick are as full as they are and continuing to get more full, is because humanity has not learned to accept this Light which it has within itself—the power of reordering the universe if need be. Individuals accept the appearance, then they become prey to the illness—usually it begins in the feelings, as you know—and then the disease. Germs rise up, though they are there all the time they suddenly begin to have power, and presently the individual gives power to them and he becomes ill. He recognizes darkness instead of Light.

Make no mistake about it, dear ones, because We tell you these things does not mean disease is not here. Because the individual hypnotizes himself into accepting less than perfection does not mean that the individual is fooling or making it all up. Humanity has been killing itself off at a great rate for lo these many centuries, because it gives power to the appearance world. Individuals must recognize God and practice God and live by God's Laws at all times, and that takes application. It takes energy. Energy you have given to appearances in the past must be offset by energy released in the other direction. Think! Through all these centuries humanity has given power to believing that it was doomed. Do you wonder humanity sits at the crossroads of eternity, that civilization faces extinction! It is because human beings individually have failed to recognize the power of God and their own responsibility to that Light.

Q. Vitamins.

A. The word "vitamin" and the use of the word, and the so-called substance of vitamins has been rather an amusing one to Me for some time. Blessed ones, those substances which individuals have found in certain foods and have given alphabetical letters and numbers to are merely the substance of life itself and can be found practically anywhere in practically anything. The great joke is that humanity likes to be reassured and so humanity will go rushing enmasse to the drug store to buy vitamins A through D, E, F, etc. just to be certain that they will have the proper vitamins, which they would undoubtedly have if they called to their Presence, and then went to work. The pill industry has become a major industry, and you may be certain it is possible to enjoy a very full and effective life without using them!

Now I should like to say something else as long as we have started on this matter of diet. Dear ones, for goodness sake, all of you eat the proper food. You cannot afford now to eat either too much or too little, and you cannot afford to fill your stomachs full of material that is too heavy for you to handle. I hope I do not have to say more about that. Blessed ones, for your own sake, turn to your Presence. Use your good sense about what you eat and how you prepare it. And you may be very certain that if your foods are properly prepared they can be simply and tastefully presented and you will not have to have a little dish of vitamin pills on the side. There are those who persist in not eating the proper foods. Naturally they have to pay the consequences, and if they don't take vitamin pills they will take something else. Well, that is one of the unfortunate things. Call your Presence into action and rely on that. Don't be afraid of vitamin pills, they certainly won't hurt you. Don't over season things. Don't under season things. Don't be fanatic about these things. Remember, you are related to this great Presence of life. Don't start putting things into your stomach you can't imagine Me eating, but for goodness sake don't go off and become fanatical about it. One of the finest statements concerning food was made by your great Friend, Jesus, when He said: "It is not what you put into your mouth that defiles you, but what comes out of your mouth." Be the master of your diet, don't be mastered by it, and don't worry about the pills!

Q. Difference between feeling and emotional worlds.

A. One is the activity of the human, the other is the activity of the divine. The *feeling world* is the world whose center is the heart and from which flows the feeling of love, of happiness, of generosity, and all the Arisen Master qualities which operate at the level of the heart. The *emotional world* is the world whose center is the solar plexus and from it pour forth the emotions of hate, anger, jealousy, criticism, and the qualities which are far from the Arisen Master octave—in other words, the opposite. Thus you will see that the two, while both capable of releasing the same type of energy, are as far apart as the poles, for one is human and the other is divine.

Q. Higher Metal Body; the seven centers in the body.

A. The activity of the Higher Mental Body does not have

an actual focus in the physical body. The Higher Mental Body is the discriminating, selective intelligence which stands between the I AM Presence and your own physical form, and there is no connection, that is, no center of the Higher Mental Body located in the physical body. However, there are two mental worlds, which is what you are referring to. The one mental world, which is the higher mental world, has its center in the front part of the brain, the part just behind the frontal bone, and there it is that the Arisen Master ideas and the promptings from the I AM Presence are received and recorded. The pineal gland in the brain is the contact point with the I AM Presence and does not have to do with the individual's thought processes; it is rather a receiving station for the inflowing energy of Light. The spleen is the center for the so-called lower mental world and it is through the activity there that thoughts of destruction are generated by the human consciousness.

There are seven principal centers in the physical body. I have already explained the activity of five of them, including the pineal gland. There are two other centers in the body—one of them is the throat, and the throat center is the center of the world of creation for the individual, for it is through the voice that the individual in physical embodiment is able to put his thought and his feeling together to bring forth the created object, whatever it may be, at the inner or the outer levels. Thus you will see that the throat is your power center for from there flows the energy of creation, and when the individual will call the Presence into action and raise all from the center of the heart, the center of the throat, and the center of the head into the pineal gland, he will live in a world of Joy and Beauty.

The seventh center is, of course, the center of pro-creation, for it is the opposite of the center of creation. It is the three lower centers which drag mankind down into the depths. The center of procreation has nothing whatever to do with creation and it is time mankind understood the difference. Also, the release of emotion through the solar plexus or the cunning planning through the activity of the spleen in the lower mental world has nothing whatsoever to do with the divine nature in man but is wholly the activity of the beast of the human, which is the negative aspect of the individual. Only by shutting those off and raising the pure energy which many times has been directed to these centers, can the individual be free from the tremendous wheel of cause and effect, free from birth and rebirth, free from inharmony and destruction of every sort. By raising the consciousness and energy away from these three lower centers into the three higher centers, making them one with the fourth and highest center, that is the pineal gland, the individual will become one with himself and the ascension will take place, for he will merge into the Higher Mental Body and will no longer be subject to any human limitation whatsoever.

Q. The Soul.

A. The soul, as conceived by the outer world teachings, is actually the Higher Mental Body, because the outer world teachings, as distorted by the present churches, have not been able to delve any deeper into the make-up of each individual than the great Guardian Presence of the Higher Mental Body. So what they think of when they say soul, and what you think of, would not be the same and you are not speaking the same language.

The soul is often mistaken to be the Great Presence of Life. Dear ones, the I AM Presence has no other name and can never receive any other name—it must be "I AM." There is no other way of describing it; there is no way of telling you what it is like; it is the innermost of all Inner things. Of course, in a sense that is the soul that the outer world is groping for, but not understanding their own connection with that Great Presence, they have been misled through countless generations to the point where it has become a very mysterious and mystic belief and something not at all possible. Their imaginations have run riot, picturing a heaven and a hell, neither of which you nor I would like to be in. The activity of Universal Control is sane, and pure, and beautiful, and lovely. The only place where inharmony enters in is where the human being has free reign over his own mental activity, where, as you say, he "goes to town" to create discord—and he goes to town!

Q. Causal Body.

A. The Causal Body is the accumulation of all effect into a realm of cause. In other words, the Causal Body is the energy qualified which will be released during the life span of an individual. That great causal realm is composed entirely of those things which are Good. That Good flows out during the lifetime of the individual. By that I do not mean necessarily that it flows out during one physical embodiment, it may take hundreds of embodiments. Remember, every good deed or act is amplified many times. That good accomplishment is energy that goes into the Causal Body. That energy, while it is still held there, is also released, thus making it possible for additional Good to be done. The Causal Body is a Great Blazing Sun of Light, and once you have seen it you will never mistake it.

Q. The physical Sun.

A. The physical Sun is a Radiating Center of Light, and there are many who claim that it is hot as a result of the fact that when the Sun shines upon the Earth heat is received, but the heat comes as a result of the friction of the light passing through the Earth's atmosphere and is certainly not transmitted from the Sun to the Earth for it could not cross the void. Anyway, the friction and the heat takes place right here. The Sun is not burning up. It is a Radiating Center of Light for this universe. It has reached a certain stage of expansion, which same state of expansion must be accomplished by every planet that exists. Science has concluded that the planets have been broken off from the Sun and whirled out into space. The truth is that the planets will eventually become suns or else come together in one Central Sun to form a much larger one, for out of the Light has come all creation and back into that Light will all creation return.

Q. The Great Central Sun.

A. The Great Central Sun is to the entire Universe what your own physical Sun is to this solar system. There is at the center of this universe a Great Body of Light so vast that your human consciousness cannot in any way conceive of the size of it. It is out of this Light that all things have come, and it is into it that they will all go. The Great Central Sun contains the original Cause, the original impulse for creation. It is through this that God has worked for countless millions of years to express Love and to bring Order and an expression of Love in order throughout space. The Great Central Sun is inhabited by transcendent Beings of Light whose work it is to decree the cosmic destiny of each planet, of each star or sun, and They thus control the expansion of the Light throughout the universe. This Great Central Sun is expanding rapidly and the radiation from It is also expanding. The entire universe in which you live is expanding at a prodigious rate and that is why your Earth must now be raised in consciousness, in vibratory action, so that it too can expand into its rightful place.

Q. Proper call for a suicide.

A. The calls for one who has committed suicide is to call first to your Presence, then to the Presence of the individual who has passed over. Call for the assistance of any one of the Masters—I will be glad to come Myself, Leto has given a great deal of service, also Jesus, and many others. Any of Us will always be glad to help in this instance. Make the call that the individual be awakened to the reality of where he is and how he got there, and then call that the Master assist him out of that condition into the realm of Light.

Respecting those who feel that they are responsible for the suicide of another, illumine them, make the call to the Presence to charge them with the understanding that no human being can ever completely take charge of another. If such responsibility has been taken, let them call for the Fire of Forgiveness, and remember, no matter how serious the offense may appear to be, at Our level all errors are as one. No one error is of necessity worse than another. A slight error is as much an error as a great error, and if the individual wishes to erase it, it will be dissolved in the Fire that dissolves all wrong, all discords; but the desire must be in the heart, it cannot be a desire of the head. When an individual is sincere from the heart all things are possible.

Q. Astrology

A. The activity of astrology and astronomy have often been confused and mankind is somewhat confused with that. The ancient study which was performed centuries ago concerning astrology was to tune into the radiation of various Masters radiating to this planet. These emanations from Great Cosmic Beings were frequently interpreted as coming directly from certain planets and when the activity seemed to bode ill then the emanation from that planet was considered to be a direful one. When the emanation appeared to bring peace or good tidings, happiness, and joy, that was considered to be helpful.

Thousands of centuries ago man became aware of the Masters, but the majority, not knowing them as Masters, presumed them to be planets, and presuming this, attributed to these planets qualities and qualifications which can influence the life of the individual.

Now, dear ones, the truth is this: The Masters radiate those qualities which the Earth requires and there are some Whose duty and privilege it is to radiate corrective measures. When an individual sees fit to stray from the true pathway and finds himself in the wrong place, he gets himself spanked. This spanking no one enjoys, and thus the individual thinks he is under malevolent influences, he was born under an unlucky star, that this has happened as a result of being born in the wrong time at the wrong place.

The Law is, dear ones, and never forget this: There is no power in heaven or earth that will stand beside the Power of your great Presence of Life. There is no predestination. There is no punishment that comes to you because the day happens to be Sunday. There is nothing coming from God except what is Good! The planets do not have influence over you, and where the radiation is powerful, the Masters are radiating something required. And there you have the explanation of astrology in its true light. Do not put faith in those things. Place your faith in God, the Great Presence of Life within you. Know it! Accept it as authoritative; then you will go forward with the speed of Light and nothing will interfere with you.

Q. The Great Pyramid.

A. The Great Pyramid of Egypt was erected a good many years ago as you reckon time—a good many years before even that civilization that you call the Atlantean civilization. It has been there a long time, and as a matter of fact, is the original pyramid from which the ideas of pyramids were copied by various peoples and civilizations from time to time. Now you would never guess who built the first one! O there are quite a number of archeologists who claim to know, but so far they are all wrong. I am going to let you guess a little more on that. A good many individuals have tried to establish, in their study of this pyramid, that the nature of the pyramid in itself was prophetic, and indeed it is, but human beings making the studies so far have missed the important key, and so their findings concerning the Great Pyramid are inaccurate and will be for some time to come.

Q. Armageddon.

A. Let Me assure you, dear ones, that even though many prophecies have been given down through the centuries that there would be the great battlefield of Armageddon, that there would be a final war, a final destruction as foretold in *Revelation*, before this great millennium would be ushered in; dear ones, I want you to know unmistakably that the thoughts and feelings of humanity which accept those prophecies are the things which help to bring those prophecies into fulfillment. It is up to you and others in the Light whom We work with, to use a cleaner, sharper weapon than prophecy. You must use the Sword of Truth! You may rest assured, dear ones, that were you able tonight to contact with sufficient power the feeling and thought world of humanity for only a few moments you could prevent the battle of Armageddon, a final religious war, and the tremendous destruction which has been foretold in *Revelation, Washington's Vision,* etc.

AFFIRMATIONS FROM THE VARIOUS MASTERS

I AM the Christ, the son of the living God, I AM,
I and the Father are one.
I AM the supplying treasure house of the Universe
flooding forth to mankind.

Make me, O I AM Presence, a mighty Sun of Light, a
mighty Sun of Freedom, a mighty Sun of Love, Wisdom
and Power, that I may be a pillar of sustaining force to
assist mankind this day.

Let Thy will, not mine be done. Make me, O Great I
AM Presence, that which I AM, that which I was in the
beginning. I accept now the Full Christ Light enfolding
me. I give no power to human creation and ever abide in
Thy great glorious Heart of Love to render my assistance, my service to mankind everywhere.

I AM the Presence, the I AM that I AM, the Presence
of Life everywhere forever. I AM that Presence, the very
essence of Life, which flows through my feeling world
and then flows on to bless, to heal, to strengthen, to
inspire. I AM the Light! Before the Dazzling Brightness of
my Inner Self all darkness flees. I AM the Eternal One,
the Quenchless Flame, the Everlasting Sun. I AM all
things.

I AM the Presence that puts aside all activity of fear, not only in my world but in the world of all with whom I come in contact.

I AM the Presence of Confidence charging forth now that mankind may acknowledge these qualities and go forward into the New Golden Age.

Peace, be still, and know that I AM God, the Full Power of Light in Action in my being and world, forever sustained by the constant expanding flow of Light from the Great Central Sun.

I AM the pure Essence of God Life enfolding me, flowing through me, and raising me into the conscious Understanding of all things.

O Great Wondrous I AM Presence, come forth! accomplish these things for me. Take out of my world these things which are impure, these things which are old human habits, these doubts, these fears, these fallings short of perfection. Replace them with your limitless substance and Power of Light, charged with the Consciousness of the Arisen Masters.

I AM the Fire Breath of Creation.
I AM the great Fire Breath illumining my entire being to the Arisen form.

I AM humble. I AM Obedient. I AM determined to be the Light. I AM determined to go forth Master on Earth!

I accept the Purifying Power in every atom of my being, cleansing me of all things that interfere. I AM now a Pure, Harmonious channel. I AM the pristine flow of Light of my own Great Radiant God-self taking complete command of my system and fulfilling its purpose.

O Great I AM, cleanse and purify my desires. See that I desire only Thy Perfection and the Perfection of the Arisen Masters.

I AM the Presence of pure desire filling my world and the world of every human being everywhere.

I AM the full Power of Light in action, filling my mind, my being, my world, then flooding forth into the world of all mankind; for I AM the action of Life, I AM the Presence of Life, I AM the Victory of Life now and forever.

I AM the Power of Divine Love filling the hearts and minds of mankind everywhere and releasing to them the Sustaining Power of Life in Action in their beings and worlds.

I AM the Conquering Presence moving into this condition with the full Power of Light in action.

I AM the Mighty Conquering Presence moving in and through all conditions that face me, sweeping the pathway clear, making victory after victory until I win my final attainment, the Ascension.

I AM the Commanding Presence sweeping in and creating Perfection in that which is to be done.

I AM the Victorious Presence of God, of Life, sweeping into my world. I AM Victorious in all that I do. I AM Master of my world.

I AM Illumined Obedience.
I AM that Obedience to the God Principle within me.

I AM the Presence of Good, knowing all things, thinking all things, being all things which are constructive.

I AM the Full Power of Light and Love.

I AM God's Power speaking through my voice.

I AM Master of all things I survey.

I AM the power of Harmony, the power of Love in action.

Give a Blessing to everybody in_____ (city)

I AM perfect opportunity at all times.

I Will! I AM! I Do!

I AM that Radiant Christ Self in action sustained.

I AM the Power that controls my feeling world, that harmonizes all things, and that keeps me charged with the feeling of Confidence, with the feeling of Courage, with the feeling of Dominion.

I AM the Projected Consciousness of the Arisen Master I am to be.

Be Still and know that I AM Master here.

I AM the Conquering Presence moving forward and bringing about the perfect condition in my world at all times.

I AM all Love and therefore I AM all things. I AM that I AM.

I AM qualifying all things with Light and love.

I AM Light! Light! Light!

I AM Love! Love! Love!

I AM God! God! God!

I AM that I AM that I AM.

I AM all things that I wish to be. I AM my Life, my Joy, my Love.

I AM the Eternal, the Everlasting, the All-enfolding

Flame of Life which is One with all things, the Infinite, the Eternal.

Thou great I AM, Thou Supreme Source of All Life, I acknowledge only Thee and give to Thy keeping my Life, my energy, my substance, which is only Thine. Henceforth there is only Thee.

Into Thy hands, my Father, do I give all things.

I AM that which I wish to become.
I AM the Fulfillment of my destiny here on Earth.
I AM the Victory of Light Itself.
I AM the Commanding Presence moving in and Conquering everywhere I move.
I AM the Victory of Life over death.
I AM that I AM.

*   *   *

I AM the Commander of my own destiny.
I AM the Conquering Presence which fills my world with the assurance of my I AM self.
I AM the Voice of God speaking through God's lips.
I AM the humble, calm, beautiful, magnificent child of Light.
I AM able now to bring forth every Good and Perfect thing that I require.
I now accept my Oneness with that of the I AM Presence, and accepting that Oneness, I move forward to be the Fulfillment of my every decree.

INDEX

Cataclysms, Do not fear cataclysms, wars, accidents, or destructive activities of the human, 80; Forces of elements unleashed upon portions of mankind that refuse to obey God's Law, 164; See Armageddon.

Causal Body: is the accumulation of all effect into a realm of cause, 207.

Christ, You are the Christ, the only begotten son of your own God Self, 127.

Claim, You will never reach the Arisen state unless you claim it for yourself, 77; You must claim a thing before you can have it, 109.

Colors, 193.

Competition: There is no, 75; See Oneness.

Confidence, Have confidence in yourself, 103.

Consciousness: Seven Stages of, 46.

Creation, "Your Power To Create," Chapter XII, 115.

Criticism: See Judgment, Gossip.

Deceit, Never try to deceive one another, 137.

Decree, Better to make one really sincere, determined call than to make fifty half-hearted attempts, 52; In calling to the Presence, do not feel that physical effort is needed, 55; Visualize the thing you call for, 59; No longer the part of wisdom to use the words "blast," "annihilate," 108.

Dependability, Learn to be true to your word even in small things, 192.

Desire, The individual who refuses to govern his desire has released destruction upon himself, 17-8; You must be above all desire to take authority. You must be above all desire to take offense, 41-2; It is only in the heart that the desire of the individual can be made pure, 102.

Discretion, You must learn not to discuss the laws which you know with those who do not believe, 112.

Discipline, Self-discipline is the only type of discipline that can exist in the New Golden Age, 75.

Hell, There is no hell other than that which you create for yourself, 184-5; See Mistakes.

Help, The Masters can help you, but only to the extent that your are able to help yourself, 67; When you help others you help yourself, 118-9.

Higher Mental Body: Is the Guardian Angel of each individual, 200; The discriminating selective intelligence which stands between the I AM Presence and your physical form, 204-5.

Hilarion: Chapter IX by, 92.

Honesty, As you value your progress be honest with life, 30.

Humility, The greater the power an individual has in his use, the greater humility there should be, 24; Seek how you may be the most humble, 68; Assistance given in all humbleness is always a God activity, 81.

I AM, The I AM instruction is the highest pinnacle of illumination and love upon this planet, 15, 128; To say "I AM" is to release the Full Power of Light throughout the universe, 22; "You are the I AM Presence," Chapter XIII, 123; The Great Creative Words, 128; Your Password into or out of any situation, 194.

Ideals: Maintain the highest possible, 37.

Imperfection, To observe imperfection in another is a certain indication you yourself have not reached the goal, 23.

Innocence, "Innocence—A Protection," Chapter XX by the Goddess of Innocence, 172; Individuals of innocent motive will be protected automatically by the Great Cosmic Law, 172-3.

Inspiration, 68-9.

Jesus: Chapter XVI by, 145; Statements by: I AM the Open Door which no man can shut, 96; Love thine enemies, 142; It is not what you put into your mouth that defiles you, but what comes out of your mouth, 204.

Judgment, Do not pass judgment, but give of your love to individuals, 176.

Karma, What you release comes back to you, 64; Sixty percent of that which you send forth remains to act within you, 119; See Forgiveness, Fire of.

Selfishness, You are not selfish just because you command and demand perfection for yourself, 158.

Serapis Bey: Chapter VII by, 74.

Service, In service one should lose himself so completely that he becomes selfless, 18; You do not help another unless you teach him to help himself, 31-3; Man must realize that he has come forth on this planet to serve, 129; All you have to do is live this Law, 183.

Silence, The first rule has always been to be silent and know that I AM is God, 21; There is nothing more important than the stilling of oneself, 28, 37; "True Silence," Chapter XI, 107; Silence not only of the spoken word, but of the thoughts and feelings, 113.

Sincere, When your desire is sincere in helping another, the way is open, 28; Be sincere in the release of the Light, 61.

Solar Plexus, Center of the emotional world, 45.

Speech, Speak clearly and distinctly and always speak with great love, 95; You must master your tongue, 112; Speak from your heart, 151-2; It is not what you put into your mouth that defiles you, but what comes out of your mouth, 204.

Stairway to Mastery, Chapter V, 49.

Suicide, Proper call for a suicide, 208.

Sun, Great Central: Is to the entire Universe what your own physical Sun is to this Solar System, 208.

Teacher: Role of a, 115.

Thought, What you say, think, and feel, you decree into your world, 58; A thought form called into action is a tangible thing, 83-5; Learn to think with accuracy and feel with accuracy, 94; See Feeling.

Throat: Is your power center, 205.

Time, There is no time, actually there is only *now*, 31.

Tolerance, Always be tolerant, 40.

Truth: Does not belong to one group of people, to one sect, to one nation, 14-6; The truth will set you free, 18; Obedience to this Law will quickly prove the truth of it, 168-9.

♥♥♥♥♥♥♥♥♥♥♥♥♥♥♥♥♥♥♥♥♥♥♥♥♥♥♥

An Invitation

from friends of Pearl Publishing

We hope you have been inspired by this book. Pearl Publishing is an organization devoted to spreading the *Ascended Masters'* teachings. If you would like to know more about this great teaching, you may choose from the following books available from Pearl Publishing. Simply write us and we would be delighted to send them to you.

Step By Step We Climb (Volume 1). Twenty-four Ascended Master Discourses by Jesus, Saint Germain and other ascended masters. ISBN 0-9619770-1-9 (pbk.)

Step By Step We Climb To Freedom (Volume 2). Continuing instruction by the Ascended Masters in the great laws of life. ISBN 0-9619770-2-7 (pbk.)

Step By Step We Climb To Freedom and Victory (Volume 3). A collection of inspirational talks by Pearl which came as a result of deep attunement to the raised consciousness of the Christ principle. Pearl's insight and sincere application of these laws provide a simple explanation of the path to mastery. ISBN 0-9619770-3-5 (pbk.)

"I AM" the Open Door. Fourteen discourses by various Ascended Masters given to Peter Mt. Shasta. ISBN 0-9619770-5-1 (pbk.)

Pearl Publishing
of Mount Shasta

P.O. Box 1290
Mount Shasta, California 96067

♥♥♥♥♥♥♥♥♥♥♥♥♥♥♥♥♥♥♥♥♥♥♥♥♥♥♥